Think Like A God

The African American Theory of Consciousness

Sean XLG Mitchell

Acknowledgements

Special thanks to Olatokunbo Babatunde Odeyemi and the Yoruba translation of mind, body, and soul (okan, ara and emi)! I would also like to thank my family beginning with Z'Kema, Safiya, Khalfani, Shannon Bland, and Stephen Pegram and to the rest of my family, friends, and fans for your support.

Special thanks to my Philadelphia connection; my brother and sister in struggle Aaron and Han. To my cousin Wanda Mitchell and the Fort, Lauderdale crew and to my DC, NC, and NY family as well.

Finally, special thanks to Tony Browder and the IKG Cultural Resource Center and Dr. Ama Mazama and Afrocentricity International.

Think Like A God: The African American Theory of
Consciousness

By Sean XLG Mitchell

Published by:
ALB Management and Publishing Co.
A Division of Team Sean XLG
Fort Washington, MD
albmngt@gmail.com
M. Mitchell, Editorial Director
S. Mitchell, Associate Publisher
Chris Howard, Associate Editor
The Printed Page, Interior Design / Cover Layout

A Word from the Author

For 400 years we were taught that Christopher Columbus discovered America. Imagine that for just a moment. Native Americans were already here but their presence seemed to have been dismissed as if their lives did not matter. They were the subject of someone else's "discovery". Evidence that Africans arrived in the Americas long before Columbus has never been given serious consideration because it does not align with the agenda of white supremacy.

To say that modern civilization began with the Greeks and not the Africans of ancient Egypt (Kemet), a much older civilization the Greeks learned from and copied, is a deliberate attempt at distorting history in the interest of European people. To assume that out of the millions who walked the earth before Newton that no one threw a rock in the air and realized that it came back down. No one else saw an apple fall from a tree but him. In other words, Newton did not discover the law of gravity as much as he may have scientifically defined it as propaganda for the powers that be.

People seem to fear and respect modern science as if it were a sanctified field. Science assumes that all living things are biological machines to include people, animals, plants, etc. It assumes that mind and consciousness are byproducts of a complex mechanical brain. Nevertheless, this determination comes from a field that believes a "big bang" created the earth but cannot adequately explain how an immense amount of heat can produce a planet that is 70% water.

African Americans have our own school of thought, theories and systems of belief that are rooted in our ancient traditions. We embrace the concepts of Nommo, Ma'at and Afrocentricity and hold our scholars in high regard. It is their historical accounts, evidence, and body of work that we cite and regard as truth.

This is not an agenda of Black supremacy. In fact, such a thing does not exist. We neither have the power nor the intent to capture, rule and oppress the world or to impose our beliefs on others as the Europeans have done. Quite the opposite, this is our voice of freedom that we are expressing after centuries of oppression. We are no longer the servants of others. We are taking our rightful place at the table of humanity as equals with dignity and respect.

There has long been a narrative that says African people are limited in our thinking. It has been said that we are "children" in terms of how we act and behave and in our understanding of things. That we have been defined in the context of struggle for so long that we have nothing tangible or very little to offer the world intellectually. Sure, we can sing, dance, run and play ball exceptionally well but what do we bring to the table as far as constructive thinking, critical analysis, and verifiable conclusions?

The African genius may have been dormant for quite some time because of African people being dislocated and moved off our cultural terms, but it started awakening with Toussaint and the Haitian Revolution. It was evident in the forming of Black Wallstreet and in the masterful works of Woodson's "The Miseducation of the Negro" and George G.M. James' "Stolen Legacy: Greek Philosophy is Stolen Egyptian Philosophy".

The African genius was there when Dr. Karenga developed Kwanzaa, Asante defined Afrocentricity along with Akbar and Noble's emergence of Black Psychology. We saw it when Diop magnificently penned "The African Origins of Civilization" and in

Van Sertima's monumental work "They Came Before Columbus: the African Presence in Ancient America". A new vision for our people came about because of innovative ideas and brilliant concepts as we began speaking our own cultural truth.

The theory of consciousness is an intellectual discourse that is rooted in classical African traditions. For example, in Kemet we had a belief in the healing rods, the source that rejuvenates and balances the body's internal energy. In Voudon, we have a belief in the power of suggestion and in an ever-present spirit and divine essence that encompasses all things. In the Odu Ifa, we have the ethical teachings of a positive worldview. Thus, the theory of the mind incorporates the crux of our ancient beliefs as a modern-day concept of a metaphysical reality.

Table of Contents

Introduction

The University of Phoenix aired a popular commercial on television not too long ago where a middle-aged, heavyset man sits in front of the camera and tells the story of a woman named Carmen Bravo. He describes her as a "first generation American" and adds that she "rose to beat the odds". She earned her master's degree and became a doctor. As a medical student, she was running in a marathon and saved the life of a man who collapsed behind her from cardiac arrest and he reveals himself as the man she saved.

Most people who watch this commercial would not think twice about it. They will simply see it as an advertisement for the University of Phoenix. Aside from a feel-good story, they really could not grasp the significance of the event as it is being detailed on TV. But from an understanding of consciousness, there is a far deeper meaning and implication. By the time you finish reading this material hopefully you will know exactly what I am talking about.

But let me start by saying that I am not a doctor. I have no medical training as a physician or as a scientist for that matter. Therefore, my viewpoints and perspectives throughout this work are not intended to be used as a substitute for either field. I am a metaphysical spiritualist. As such, I have views that are unconventional by present standards but essentially my work applies an ancient philosophical approach to a modern-day reality.

This is to say that if modern man had all the answers, we would not have any problems. The idea that we live in a world where most people are on some form of medication suggests that we live in a "sick" society. Very few people can be considered as being healthy because healthy people do not require medication. But we live in a day and time where there is a pill for everything, and the pharmaceutical industry is a multi-billion-dollar business.

What we think of as being real is typically nothing more than an abstract perception. In other words, our lives often center around superficial things such as money, material possessions, entertainment, recreation, shopping, debt, taxes, and death. There is very little room for personal and collective growth and development. Music and television are primarily for enjoyment and offers little to nothing for the mind and soul. We use prayer as a casual activity but not as a true spiritual expression in terms of consciousness.

But metaphysics doesn't have all the answers either. In fact, most of what we present in terms of possibility is no more than a theory. The reason for this is because it is a new emerging field of study that has yet to fully develop with case studies, experiments, and extensive data to support its argument. Its premise may be ancient, but the current model is still in its infancy.

Metaphysical concepts undoubtedly have rough edges that need to be refined, smoothed out and sharpened. I would be amiss if I suggested otherwise. So, what I am attempting to present here is a body of work that hinges on creative logic and techniques with informational support. I have quite a bit of research material with a heavy reliance on professional opinions from various sources.

At the end of the day, however, a metaphysical reality goes against the grain. People have become accustomed to believing what they experience as truth which is interpreted by a highly influenced scientific definition and understanding. On the other hand, you have some people who stand on the side of theology. They utilize scriptures for what they believe to be truth and anything that cannot be substantiated by passages is a false belief. So, the metaphysical theorist stands alone.

For centuries, many countries around the world embraced an esoteric practice but what is new today is no longer a part of the ancient world. This is the reality that I am here to challenge. It begins with the simple idea of mind over matter. Anyone who has ever fantasized about sex can attest to the fact that a thought alone can change the body's physiology in terms of being physically aroused. Now apply this concept to all other areas of life experiences when it comes to our thoughts and the mind-body connection.

Because what if there is more to the world than what science and religion has to offer? What if there is more to the human experience than what we have been led to believe? And what if there is more to the reality around us that we have yet to comprehend? We are going to take this general concept and move it forward beyond the boundaries of our self-imposed limitations. Welcome to the bata drum!

The Idea of Consciousness

In the Journal of Projective Techniques in 1957, Dr. West was treating Mr. Wright who had an advanced stage of lymphosarcoma, a rare form of cancer. Mr. Wright had tumors the size of oranges all over his body to include his neck, chest, abdomen, arm pits and groin, and his cancer was causing milky fluid to build up in his chest every day, making it hard for him to breathe. All treatments had failed, and he was not expected to last beyond a week.

Mr. Wright desperately wanted to live, and he hung his hope on a new promising drug called Krebiozen which had only been used in clinical trials but according to his doctor he was too sick to qualify. Mr. Wright refused to give up, believing Krebiozen was his miracle cure, he continued to persist in requesting the drug until Dr. West gave in. Dr. West injected him with the drug on a Friday and on the following Monday, his patient was walking around out of bed.

Mr. Wright's tumors had "melted like snowballs on a hot stove" and were half their original size. Ten days after the first dose of Krebiozen, Mr. Wright left the hospital, apparently cancer free. Mr. Wright praised Krebiozen as a miracle drug for two months until scientific literature began publishing reports that Krebiozen did not seem to be effective. Mr. Wright trusting what he read in the literature, fell into a deep depression, and his cancer returned.

This time Dr. West decided to trick Mr. Wright by telling him the initial supplies of the drug had deteriorated during shipping, making them less effective, but he received a new batch of highly concentrated, ultra-pure Krebiozen, which he could give him. Dr. West then injected Mr. Wright with nothing but distilled water and a miraculous thing happened-again. The tumors melted away, the chest fluid disappeared, and Mr. Wright was feeling great once more.

For the next two months, Mr. Wright was on cloud nine. His cancer had gone into remission a second time and he was enjoying his life cancer free. Then the American Medical Association announced a nationwide study of Krebiozen proved that the drug was completely worthless. This time, Mr. Wright lost all faith in his treatment. His cancer came back, and he died two days later.

This is one of many stories I came across when I began to study the mind-body connection over 20 years ago. In my attempt to understand how a conscious belief works, I discovered some interesting information on the general subject of cancer. Curiously, I ventured into this arena because this has been a highly publicized health issue for years. I also have an aunt who is a breast cancer survivor, a friend who underwent a double mastectomy and family members who have succumbed to the disease.

Breast cancer, for instance, according to statistics affects one in eight women in America but surprisingly it is a rather recent epidemic. In 1970, there were a moderate 68,000 cases reported in the U.S. However, by 2014, there had been a staggering 242 percent jump. The spike in female breast cancer rates have been more than 4-fold. In addition, colon/rectal cancer and cigarette-related lung cancer in women significantly increased over the same time span.

The rise in rates in the last 50 years were abrupt and the tragic epidemic continues as evidenced by the number of new cases at the beginning of each of the previous six decades: 1970

(68,000), 1980 (110,000), 1990 (150,000), 2000 (182,800), 2010 (207,090), and 2020 (276,480). This trend represents an alarming rate of increase in the American breast cancer epidemic and has clearly become more common in the United States since the last half century. But the burning question is why?

Since 1985, there has been an ongoing public campaign concerning breast cancer. Women have been educated about the importance of annual mammograms and have been encouraged to do self-exams for early detection. There's national organizations and movements such as the American Cancer Society, Susan G. Komen, pink ribbons, and breast cancer awareness month. Medical science and treatments have advanced over the years, billions of dollars have been raised for research, and despite an upsurge in public awareness 40,000 women continue to die each year.

While most people would view this as a health crisis, in studying the mind-body connection it can equally be viewed as a crisis in consciousness. In other words, the more the movement became popular the more the cases that were being diagnosed. A parallel growth was taking place. While they thought the attention would reduce the numbers it may have caused them to increase. Although the medical world is perplexed and at a loss regarding these statistics, consciousness may be able to explain this phenomenon.

When mass media generates a host of news stories, commercials, and articles about breast cancer it puts a spotlight on the disease and plants a seed of possibility in the minds of women. This is in addition to annual mammograms and ongoing conversations women have with their doctor, family and friends about their exams and results. It is the fear and anxiety of looking in the mirror every day or taking a shower and wondering "is that a lump". It is constantly thinking about the aunt, mother or sister who was just diagnosed and asking yourself if it runs in the family.

What happens when the mind is consumed in thought and that thought is predicated on fear? And what happens when the mind is under stress when it receives this overwhelming information? In which direction does the scale tilt? As we saw in the story of Dr. West, not only did a conscious belief determine the fate of his cancer patient but it raises a very intriguing question. If a state of mind can determine the outcome of a cancer diagnosis how much does it affect the onset of the disease?

To demonstrate how powerful a thought can be, during medical studies placebos, fake drugs (sugar pills) and sham procedures such as needles that retract instead of injecting, have cured and/or relieved migraine headaches, irritable bowel syndrome and lowered blood pressure in patients who were led to believe their treatments were real. In one clinical study involving hotel maids, it reduced body fat and resulted in weight loss. According to a Harvard health article, "under the right circumstances, a placebo can be just as effective as traditional treatments".

In 2007, Dr. Roy Reeves reported a near fatal case of "Mr. A" who was suffering from depression when he consumed an entire bottle of pills. After regretting his decision, he rushed to the emergency room and collapsed in the reception area. He appeared to be in grave condition as his blood pressure had plummeted and he was hyperventilating.

He was immediately given intravenous fluids but during his examination blood tests could find no trace of the drug in his system. Four hours later, another doctor arrived at the hospital to inform Reeves that Mr. A had been in the placebo arm of a drug trial and had "overdosed" on sugar tablets. Upon hearing the news, Mr. A felt relieved and recovered soon after. Although it turned out to be a false alarm, the harrowing experience that landed him in the hospital was triggered by fear, anxiety, and a conscious belief.

The Sydney Morning Herold newspaper published a story on Damien Finniss who was working as a physiotherapist, when, on one winter afternoon in 2001, he set up his treatment table in a shed at the perimeter of a Sydney footy ground. As players came off with various aches-a pulled hamstring here, a calf strain there-Finniss ministered to them with therapeutic ultrasound, a device that applies sound waves to the injured area with a handheld probe.

He was quoted in the article as saying, "I treated in excess of five or six athletes during the training session. I'd treat them for five or ten minutes and they'd say, 'I feel much better' and run back on to the training field," recalls Finniss, a medical doctor and Associate Professor at the University of Sydney's Pain Management and Research Institute at the time of the interview. "But at the end of the session, I realized that I'd, basically, had the machine turned off." He went on to say, "I've seen people who have had terrible arthritic pain for five or ten years, receive a placebo injection, stand up, and walk straight out".

Consider the following stories:

- David Seidler, who won an Oscar for best original screenplay for "The King's Speech," suffered from bladder cancer. But Seidler survived the cancer and says he did so by using the same vivid imagination he employed to write his award-winning script. He was quoted as saying "I know it sounds awfully Southern California and woo-woo," he admits when he describes the visualization techniques he used, "but that's what happened." He visualized a "lovely, clean, healthy, unblemished bladder" for two weeks, and the cancer disappeared.

- Sharyn Mackay was diagnosed with a cancerous tumor, spindle cell sarcoma, on her kidney which was so rare that doctors at Craigavon Area Hospital sent samples of it for examination by specialists in London, Glasgow, and Harvard. The mother-of-four was then dealt a further devastating blow by doctors- the cancer was inoperable and chemotherapy, even if it worked, would only prolong her life a few weeks.

  The night before her next scan she prayed and wrote in her journal: 'Thank you God for healing me. I know I will get clear results tomorrow.' The next day the cancer disappeared. She stated, "Four radiographers studied the scans and none of them could quite believe it."

- Adeline was diagnosed with uterine cancer in her early 30s; it had spread throughout her body. Her doctors recommended chemotherapy and radiation following surgery. Her chances of survival were minimal.

Unwilling to subject herself to the harsh treatment, she decided to make her last few months as peaceful as possible.

She began taking long walks in the redwoods of Northern California where she lived. She took long baths every day, and with every activity she imagined tiny glittering healing stars raining from heaven. As she envisioned, the stars passed through her body, and whenever the point of a star touched a cancer cell, she imagined it popping like a burst balloon.

In addition to her imagination, she made significant changes in her physical environment as well. She began eating healthy foods, meditating, reading inspirational books, and distanced herself from negative people. When she returned to the hospital for a checkup nine months later, Adeline's doctors could find no trace of cancer in her body.

The human body produces thousands of potential cancer cells each day that our immune system identifies and destroys on an ongoing basis. Tumors form when protective cells fail to do their job. This much is understood, but when a person with stage 4 cancer goes into spontaneous remission it completely baffles western science because they have no way of understanding or explaining how it happens. This means that on some level the human body can rid itself of disease without medical intervention.

The top 5 regions of breast cancer rates in the world:

1. Australia/New Zealand
2. Western Europe
3. Northern Europe
4. North America
5. Southern Europe

The lowest 5 regions of breast cancer rates in the world:

5. South-Eastern Asia
4. Western Africa
3. Eastern Africa
2. Middle Africa
1. South-Central Asia
   - *2019 Statistics from Susan G. Komen*

Between the two groups which regions have the more advanced healthcare systems? Which of the two are more established in terms of economic and social development? Which of the regions are better equipped in education, medical care accessibility and resources? What about the quality of food, clothing, shelter, water, proper nutrition, and sanitization? Every single advantage favors the former group over the latter and yet they have the leading cases of breast cancer in the world.

The idea that the mind controls the body may seem foreign and unrealistic to many people today but for centuries it was a common belief in many parts of the world that humans are spiritual beings who are having a physical experience. It was not until the late 14th century with the European explorations that new and differing views began to gain traction around the globe. Science became the new standard of defining reality and the mind was reduced to nothing more than a nominal activity of the brain.

Western science has projected itself as a leading authority when it comes to medicine in such a way that it's not only respected but often revered. But when you look beyond the smoke and mirrors of fancy degrees and pristine white coats, the average schoolteacher and mail carrier in Hong Kong has a longer life expectancy than a U.S. doctor by nearly ten years. This is not to say that Western science has not contributed significantly to the advancement of medicine, but no school of thought has a monopoly on truth.

To further illustrate this point, a 74-year old woman in Dublin, Ireland, had been troubled by a rash that would not go away. By the time she arrived at the hospital, her lower right leg was covered in waxy lumps, unsightly eruptions that were aggressively red and purple. Tests confirmed the worst suspicions: it was carcinoma, a form of skin cancer. Given the spread of the tumors, radiotherapy would not have been effective; nor could the doctors remove the tumors from the skin.

Amputation was considered the best option, says Alan Irvine, the patient's doctor at St. James' Hospital, but at her age she was unlikely to adapt well to a prosthetic limb. After a lengthy discussion, they decided to wait while they considered all the possible options. "We had a lot of agonizing for what to do", says Dr. Irvine. But in the meantime, she kissed a religious relic she kept with her and a "miracle" started to happen.

Despite receiving no treatment at all, the tumors were shrinking before their eyes. "We watched for a period of a few months and the tumors just disappeared," says Irvine. After 20 weeks, the patient was cancer-free. "There had been no doubt about her diagnosis," he says. "But now there was nothing in the biopsies, or the scans." He continued to add, "It shows that it is possible for the body to clear cancer-even if it is incredibly rare."

How Consciousness Creates Reality

Hillary Harris of Wisconsin was adopted when she was a little more than a month old, and as an adult she began her relentless quest to find her birth family. She explored ancestry.com as well as Facebook in hopes of discovering clues to her past. In 2012, when she was pregnant with her daughter Stella, she sought assistance from her adoption agency, Catholic Charities, for any information it could share about her birth family.

Since it was an open adoption, the agency sent her a packet of documents that included the name and obituary of her father, Wayne Clouse, who died in 2010, and the names of two half-sisters, one of which was Dawn Johnson. In the meantime, she was dealing with the distraction of a new family moving into the vacant house next door.

The new neighbors were a couple with two sons. After months of searching for houses, they were content with moving into the small cottage-style "fixer-upper". After the deal finally was completed in late June, the couple set to work on restoring their new home. At one point, Hillary and her husband Lance stopped by to introduce themselves to the new neighbors Kurt and Dawn with whom they shared a driveway.

The first hint of anything unusual came when Hillary's daughter, Stella, kept visiting the new neighbors, especially the mother, and liked to have "ready-set-go" races in the driveway. As the mother of two boys, she enjoyed the opportunity to interact with a little girl, but Hillary acknowledged her daughter's steady contact with the little-known lady next door made her uncomfortable. And although her neighbor's name was Dawn, she thought, what are the chances the woman next door could be her missing sister? Surely, that was not possible.

Hillary's search, however, for her long-lost sister came to a dramatic conclusion "that beautiful day" in August when she glanced up their shared driveway and saw a delivered stack of shingles for Dawn and Kurt, who were redoing their roof. Printed across the stack on a big red banner were the letters "J-O-H-N-S-O-N." Hillary could scarcely believe her eyes. To her the banner was confirmation that her new neighbor was "Dawn Johnson" — the sister she had been searching for. As it turns out, her father was in fact the same Wayne Clouse.

It is a remarkable true story but is it possible that it's more than just a coincidence? Although a coincidence is the first thought that comes to mind, no one would assume or dare believe that a conscious thought is what brought the two sisters together. The idea that humans have this capability makes some of us feel uncomfortable because it challenges the assumption that everything in the physical world can be explained in a common sense and practical way.

Prior to meeting my wife Z'Kema, she had committed to fasting and praying every day for one year to meet and marry her soul mate. This was her intended goal, so it became her conscious thought. I was living in a different city at the time and although we did not know each other she and I worked in the same field.

Coincidently, my oldest brother was engaged and planning his wedding and my cousin was just recently married. Since we are all close in age, I began to entertain the idea of a lifelong commitment as well even though I was single. On the day of my brother's ceremony, we changed clothes after the wedding and prepared to head over to the reception hall. While waiting, we were standing around joking and having a good time when my aunt started going on about the two weddings being so close together and how she hopes it's the last one for a while. I responded by saying that I was getting married next. She looked at me and smiled and asked when? I said in September and we all chuckled and laughed.

As the summer months were upon us, I was looking for a job that paid more money which led me to apply for several jobs, one of which was a position at Z'kema's workplace. Not only did I land that particular job, but she and I were soon introduced by a co-worker to each other, and we started dating for a short period of time and as fate would have it, we were married two months later at the justice of the peace. The irony is that we exchanged vows on the anniversary date of her one-year commitment which happened to be in September.

Over the years I have often wondered how a chain of events such as this could happen. It doesn't make sense from a logical point of view and yet it is far too detailed and neatly packaged for it to be a coincidence. As I studied similar stories throughout the years, I concluded that for a thought to go out into the world with the ability to manipulate the time, attention and actions of other people is not only beyond phenomenal but it requires a support system to map out, plan and execute the details.

It's one thing to want something, but it's a different ballgame when it comes to figuring out how you are going to receive it. For example, you can order a meal at a restaurant, but a plate of food is not going to just magically appear at your table. Someone must prepare the dish and serve it to you. And this is the process that we are focusing on. Who is the chef and server in this equation? So, there is a support system at work that we must identify and acknowledge because this is the root of a conscious reality.

We refer to this support system as "the field". When you study the field, you understand that there is more to the air we breathe than what we realize. The earth is literally a ball of energy. It is encompassed and totally immersed in it which is evident from the ever-growing grass all around us, trees, flowers, and other greenery to the illumination of the sun, moon, and stars. From oxygen in the air, and in bodies of water to periodic tracts of rain, every form of life requires a source of living energy.

Energy is unseen and yet everywhere present. It is underneath and above ground. We intake it every time we inhale and exhale, and if it transmits our conscious thoughts, then we can assume it is a form of higher intelligence. This would infer that all people are interconnected in a similar manner as a grid or a spider web effect. This means potentially, we can all be affected by the thoughts of others whether directly or indirectly.

The field responds to our thoughts by acting as a mirror to produce a reflection of our internal feelings. Whereas a conscious thought is a heightened state of awareness. When a thought is fueled by emotion it emits energy into the field as it emerges in the mind. Emotions are wide-ranging to include hope, desire, fear, anger, sympathy, etc. but once a thought takes form it begins to manifest into reality. This process works whether your thoughts are positive or negative, internal, in terms of self-development or external regarding your personal environment.

To demonstrate how powerful our thoughts are and how intricately the process works, we are going to examine real life experiences of people, grouped by profession, to illustrate how a conscious mind creates a parallel reality.

Off-duty medical personnel:

In Kissimmee, Fl., RN, Carmen Roman was at home when a driver lost control of his car and crashed into her property. She revived him and provided medical care until emergency personnel arrived.

In Philadelphia, a 16-year-old was eating at a neighborhood restaurant when he started having a heart attack. By sheer "coincidence", nurse Sarah Kane and her doctor fiancé were dining there too and saved his life.

RN, Brittany Hamstra who works in an epilepsy unit, sat adjacent to a woman on a plane who required her assistance for seizures during a flight with no medical personnel on board.

In San Jose, RN Debbie Marquez provided emergency care to an elderly man who went into cardiac arrest in a movie theater while she was watching a film.

Angela Mirador, a Washington nurse at an assisted living center, performed lifesaving CPR on her neighbor who was suffering from cardiac arrest.

Registered Nurses Katie Sloat and Deb Probst of Cascade, MI, saved the life of a man who went into cardiac arrest while giving a speech at a banquet they attended.

Nursing student, Anica Gray was driving to the university when she stopped to provide emergency aid to a man who had collapsed on the side of the road.

Registered nurse Laura Miller was on her way home from Hartford Hospital in Connecticut when she came upon an accident and saved a motorcycle crash victim.

In Syracuse, RN David Vargo saved a woman using the Heimlich maneuver who was choking while dining at a restaurant.

In Alabama, off-duty nurse Jennifer Folds was driving pass a Burger King and noticed a man lying on the pavement and stopped to perform CPR on him until paramedics arrived.

SGMC Registered Nurse, Janice Oliver was out walking with her husband around a golf course when they noticed a golfer was in medical distress and she immediately acted and saved his life.

In Ohio, Keith Ezell stopped at a crash scene on his way to the hospital to start his shift to give CPR to a pregnant woman following a serious car accident.

Mrs. Vogel, a registered nurse, and her husband were out to get food at a tavern in Florida when they noticed a woman pale and unconscious in a booth. She immediately went into action, applying a

In Wilmington, NC, an off-duty nurse helped save a 60-year-old man who collapsed while exercising at Planet Fitness.

In Weymouth, Mass., a nurse was shopping at BJ's at the same time a man was sampling meats at the deli counter and began choking. She quickly responded and saved his life.

In Ocala, Florida, RN Amy Somwaru responded to a medical emergency at an intersection while driving by and stopped to give CPR to an unresponsive man until county fire and rescue arrived.

At a suburb in Sunset Beach, a ten-year-old severed an artery in his leg from a biking accident while an off-duty nurse was jogging by and rendered lifesaving aid.

In York, Pa., Talysha Hughes, a detox nurse was with her daughter at Walmart and immediately assisted a man who was on the ground, unconscious from an opioid

CPR technique and saved her life.	overdose.

Mixed Martial Artists outside of the sport:

A few years ago, Las Vegas hosted a UFC Hall of Fame event for mixed martial artists. On the weekend of the event, former champ Matt Serra was dining in a restaurant and had to take down a drunken customer who became belligerent and began threatening the waiters. In another incident, a mma fighter involved in a road rage incident defeated two men with weapons.

In Chicago, a mma fighter beat up a gun-wielding thug who tried to carjack him, and Sergio Hernandez Jr., a black belt in Jiu-Jitsu, chased and pinned down a burglar attempting to break into his father's house in San Diego.	Renzo Gracie was followed by two men while walking to his car at 3am in Manhattan after leaving a party. After attempting to rob him, Gracie put the first guy down with two punches and the other one ran away.
Mixed martial artist Tara LaRosa took down and restrained an angry protester who bit her at a flag waiving event in Portland.	Top contender, Polyana Viana left a man with severe facial injuries after he attempted to rob her in Rio de Janeiro.
In Washington, DC, a fighter had to take down and subdue another customer who threatened the manager of a CVS Pharmacy with a knife.	Nick Ring, A Canadian professional boxer and mixed martial artist, interrupted a group of teens mugging a couple at a bus stop in Canada.

MMA veteran Andy Haigh came to the aid of a police officer who was wrestling with an armed suspect on the street by placing him in a rear-naked choke.

In Wisconsin, Dan LaSavage came face to face with a home intruder who he rendered unconscious with a guillotine choke.

In Burbank, California, a would-be robber entered the Defiant MMA & Fitness studio and was disarmed and restrained by the instructor.

Popular UFC commentator, Joe Rogan, killed a mountain lion in a bizarre confrontation after leaving a night club.

In Las Vegas, former combatant, James McSweeney was shopping with his mother and sister in a store that was being robbed at gunpoint. He went into action pinning one suspect down while the other one fled the scene.

In Las Cruces, N.M., Joe Torrez defended his home and family against four gang members, killing one assailant and severely injuring another.

In New Jersey, Jon Jones, on the morning of a title fight, apprehended a thief he witnessed steal a GPS system from a car and run off.

Light heavyweight competitor Anthony Smith used his skills and fought off a home intruder at his residence in Nebraska.

Combatant Jose Cortes overcame an attack in broad daylight while walking down the street in West Palm Beach, Florida.

A pair of mma fighters in town for a tournament in California spoiled a robbery at the motel where they were staying by disarming the suspect who held a 9mm handgun on the clerk at the front desk.

In Las Vegas, at 3:45 in the afternoon, an off-duty officer was driving his personal car when a vehicle tried to cut him off. In escalating an incident of road rage, the driver then pulled up next to the officer's driver side window and shot at him several times. In Georgia, Ruth Stringer, a lieutenant with the Dekalb County Sheriff's Office, was preparing for a five-mile run before she apprehended a suspect for attempting to kidnap a 13-year-old girl.

In Philadelphia, off-duty police officer Jason Santiago was in plainclothes when he confronted and shot a man on the street who attacked him with a pair of scissors.

Officer John O'Rourke was on the way to his wedding when he stopped at a doughnut shop in Florida and saved a 3-year-old suffering from a seizure.

In south San Francisco, police shot and killed a man who went on a rampage stabbing a customer and an off-duty officer at a gas station.

An off-duty Colorado Springs officer fatally shot a man who got into his personal car at a fast food restaurant and claimed he had a gun.

Irvington police officer Arcangelo Liberatore was off duty with his family when he saved a 5-year-old girl from a wild coyote attack.

In Chicago, an officer who was off duty was walking to his car when he was approached by a man who tried to carjack him.

A police sergeant was home in Baltimore when he was shot multiple times while he was standing on his front lawn by a masked gunman who tried to rob him.

Off-duty LAPD cop shot and killed a man who struck him in the back of the head in an unprovoked attack while he was shopping in Costco.

In San Antonio, off-duty UCPD officer shot two teens who pointed a gun at him and threatened to kill him.	And in Missouri, a cop saved his next-door neighbor's family from a home invasion by a gunman.
In Kentucky, married officers Chase and Nicole Mckeown thwarted a robbery attempt while they were out on a date.	In Indiana, an off-duty officer shopping with his family in Walmart, stepped into action to detain a suspect after a shooting inside the store.
In Georgia, Ruth Stringer, a lieutenant with the Dekalb County Sheriff's Office, was preparing for a five-mile run before she apprehended a suspect for attempting to kidnap a 13-year-old girl.	A teen in Charlotte was shot after trying to rob an off-duty CMPD police officer Emily Bishop. The shooting happened around midnight at Waterford Square Apartments.

Off-duty firefighters:

Jeff Meffert was driving down the highway in Orange County when he noticed a small two engine airplane flying low in his direction. As the plane continued to rapidly descend, he felt a thud from the impact of the aircraft as it skidded across the highway in front of him and burst into flames. Meffert maintained control of his SUV before coming to a stop and was able to run over to pull the passengers from the fiery wreckage.

In Bloomington, Indiana, Gregory Bare was home getting ready for bed when he noticed his neighbor's house on fire. He called 911, ran next door and rescued	In Alabama, Josh Brown was on his way home when he looked over to the left side of the road and saw a home on fire with smoke pouring from the windows. After calling it

two people before firefighters arrived.

In Phoenix, an off-duty firefighter is hailed as a hero after rescuing a dog from a burning home.

Roben Duge was on his way home when he saw thick black smoke pouring out of a home in Jamaica, Queens. He immediately acted and saved a grandmother and two children from certain death.

An off-duty firefighter saw smoke coming out of a burning home in Roxbury one morning and kicked in the door to rescue a woman and two birds inside.

On a highway in Massachusetts, an off-duty firefighter came across a truck that had crashed, rolled over, and was on fire with an occupant trapped inside and helped pull the man to safety.

In Franklin, Ohio, a teen lost control of a car and slammed into a tree, catching fire with the driver pinned inside. Lt.

in, he quickly responded to the scene to assist.

In Petersburg, VA, off-duty firefighter Chris Lawrence saved his 95-year-old neighbor from a house fire.

In Detroit, a woman's minivan caught on fire as she pulled into her driveway. A nearby off-duty firefighter responded by getting the homeowners out the house before the flames engulfed their property.

While on his way home after a 48- hour shift at the fire house, Nick Weichel of Elsie, Oregon, saved a couple trapped in a fiery car on an icy bridge.

In Montgomery County, Maryland, Lt. Owens was on his way to work when he spotted a massive fire consuming a home with two people inside. After calling it in, he pulled over and helped rescue the couple.

In Salem, New Hampshire, Michael Galipeau was leaving work from the fire department and was in the

Gary Zimmer was on the way to dinner with his wife when he came across the scene and rescued the man from the car. right place at the right time to save a woman from a burning car at an accident scene.

There is an obvious correlation between what people do and think in terms of their consciousness and what happens in their lives. What are the chances that firefighters are dealing with fires when they are not on duty? How about off duty police officers dealing with crime and mix martial artists having physical confrontations outside of sporting events? Are they mere coincidences or the effects of conscious thought?

The common denominator in each of the examples given is that all the individuals work in a high-stress profession. This means they carry an aura of their consciousness that is powerful enough to manipulate their personal environment. A conscious thought is amplified in a similar manner as music being played from a loudspeaker. It is far reaching and prevailing.

This is not to suggest that every time they walk out of their homes or in the public a calamity occurs. First, it does not happen to all people nor is it going to happen all the time. Secondly, no two people are the same. Two individuals can share the same experience and be affected in a completely different manner. We often see it when soldiers go to war but not everyone will suffer from PTSD years later.

To understand an elevated consciousness in descriptive terms would be like functioning at a level 8 on a 10-point scale. So, it doesn't take much for some people to be pushed to a certain point. Whereas others may leave their job and never think about work until they return the next day. However, people who are conscious often carry the weight of emotional baggage with them everywhere they go.

If we were to follow this same line of logic, we could reasonably say that some judges will develop a consciousness that centers around crime for the simple fact that they preside over criminal cases and serve as an arbiter in disputes. This would make them susceptible to similar experiences:

- In Cincinnati, Judge Susan Dlott and her husband were the victims of a home invasion
- In Detroit, a judge was robbed on her way to church by a man who told her he had a gun
- In Moultrie, GA, two men robbed Superior Court judge Brian McDaniel at his home
- In 2019, an Austin judge was ambushed outside of her home
- A Will County Judge, David Carlson was carjacked in a Chicago Greektown neighborhood
- African American judge of Los Angeles Superior Court, David Cunningham was the victim of police profiling during a traffic stop
- In 2020, a Gwinnett magistrate Judge died from injuries sustained in a hit and run accident
- A retired judge who spent two decades on the bench in Miami was robbed at gunpoint
- In 2019, a thief in Kalamazoo stole a judge's Buick Enclave after taking it for a "test drive"

There are several other cases involving thefts and stolen property, lost cash, domestic violence, and murder. In fact, three judges in Indianapolis were involved in a shooting altercation outside a fast food restaurant at 3:00 am in the morning. But there is no limitation when it comes to consciousness. The general concept applies across the board.

For instance, the person who sits at home watching television everyday will unknowingly be exposed to countless hours of healthcare commercials. They range in everything from psoriasis, shingles and joint pain to vision problems, headaches, teeth sensitivity and arthritis. After seeing an abundance of health topics, it often becomes a subject of their general conversations.

The rule of thumb is if you talk about it, it means you think about it, and if you think about it then it is on your conscious mind. As a result, they may experience ongoing health issues one after another to include aches, pain, injury, illness, disease, medications, surgeries, etc.

This is not to say that medical conditions are not real or that people are intentionally making themselves sick. But illness, like anything else, can be exacerbated or influenced to be self-induced. For example, the prostate is a medical concern for men over 50 in the U.S., but it's almost non-existent for men over 50 in other parts of the world and the difference is not necessarily as simple as diet and lifestyle.

A few general scenarios to think about:

Person A often complains about his/her food every time they eat out. They anticipate beforehand that their food order may not be correct once it arrives and because of their conscious energy they are usually correct. Either an item is missing, the food is cold, or it's not prepared right, but this becomes a pattern every time they dine out. Person A can even be with a group of people at a restaurant and may be the only one with a complaint about their meal, but it happens consistently.

Person B complains about always having bad luck and nothing ever goes right for them. Every time they turn around, they find themselves confronted with an obstacle that other people either do not have or can easily work around. They wake up recounting their problems as if they are looking for something to complain about. Nevertheless, Person B seems "trapped" with ongoing issues.

Person C just got married and the idea of being in a lifelong commitment resonates in their unconscious mind and the wedding ring serves as a daily reminder. Coincidently, he/she will run into an old ex they had not seen in years or someone on the job appears to openly flirt with them or they're stopped in the grocery store to engage in conversation with a stranger. Person C is drawing attention to themselves based on the conscious thought of their relationship status.

Person D works in the medical field as either a doctor, nurse, paramedic, etc. and they are committed to their career in the healthcare industry and often find themselves working long hours for extensive periods of time. It would be expected, then, to some degree, that someone who is close to them either a significant other, child, relative or friend will have ongoing health issues that will range from minor to major. This reality is aligned with Person D's consciousness.

Person E is a gun enthusiast and they collect weapons as a hobby. They frequently shoot at the gun range and when they are not talking about guns, they are cleaning them. It would be expected at some point for someone like Person E to be involved in a confrontation of some sort where using a firearm becomes necessary. Whether their house or car is broken in to, a family member is threatened, or someone attempts to rob them, and it may be in self-defense but that's the energy they attract.

Person F works in the field of human services supporting children or adults with disabilities. They are passionate about their work and care a great deal about the people they help every day. They become emotionally attached to certain individuals on the job and will often have conversations about them at home. In understanding consciousness, it would not come as a surprise if Person F travels out of town and consistently run into people with a disability. They may even experience a diagnosis of some sort that renders them disabled or have a child born with a disability.

These are generic examples that range from minor and moderate to extreme to help identify modes of consciousness and recognize how we create our own reality. The scenarios allow us to better understand the power of our thoughts and the mind-body connection.

Mind Over Matter

Stephen Hawking's final, posthumous book "Brief Answers to the Big Questions", details final thoughts the physicist had on the "biggest questions" humankind faces. In the book, Hawking wrote "there is no God" and expands on that premise more deeply throughout the work. He further states "The question is, is the way the universe began chosen by God for reasons we can't understand, or was it determined by a law of science? I believe the second."

Modern science is based on a theory that everything in the universe operates in a mechanical way. Those who ascribe to this materialistic belief cannot accept any evidence to the contrary regardless of how obvious and apparent it may be. The dogma assumes that all living things are biological machines, which at their core are mechanical. This includes people, animals, plants, etc. It assumes that mind and consciousness are byproducts of a complex mechanical brain.

It assumes that matter is therefore unconscious, nature has no purpose, and there is no spiritual reality to consider. Mind over matter phenomena that are not physical or measurable are therefore not provable from scientific observations. Nevertheless, this determination comes from a field that believes a "big bang", a fiery explosion in the galaxy, created earth but cannot adequately explain how an immense amount of heat can produce a planet that is 70% water. Not to mention there is no outward evidence of the earth ever being burned or scorched. Even so, how does ice revive burnt ashes?

Not all science is bad but there are realities in life that it simply cannot explain. Consider the fact that 90% of the world's population get their height from their parents. When you factor in gender, males and females usually grow within an inch or two of their father's and mother's height, respectively. While this is the norm for most people in general it is not consistent for professional basketball players where height is critical to their success.

Average height per position:

- Point Guard: 6'2"
- Shooting Guard: 6'5"
- Small forward: 6'7"
- Power Forward: 6'9"
- Center: 6'11"

NBA great Moses Malone stood at 6'10" while his father was only 5'6" and his mom stood at 5'2". Wilt Chamberlain reached 7'1" while his dad stood at 5'8", and 6'8" Celtics forward Gordon Haywood's father is 5'10". Jeremy Lin stands at 6'3" while his mom and dad are both 5'6". All-star Russell Westbrook stands at 6'3" and outgrew both of his parents by several inches. Michael Jordan, arguably the greatest NBA player of all time, stands at 6'6" while his dad was 5'9" and his mom 5'5". Science cannot account for the height variances of these professional athletes only their aspirations to play the game.

Consider what happens when war veterans who suffer from PTSD (post-traumatic stress syndrome) are alerted by a loud noise. Any sound from a firecracker explosion to a car backfiring can trigger an emotional response in former military combatants that produces the same physiological reaction, i.e., anxiety, adrenaline rush, rapid heart rate, etc., as if they were reliving the experience on a battlefield. And yet, this extreme reaction is from a simple thought in the form of a memory.

Let us consider a Stanford University study that suggests just thinking that you are prone to a given outcome may trump the argument of both nature and nurture. In fact, simply believing a physically reality about yourself can nudge the body in that direction-sometimes even more than being prone to the reality, according to the results. The researchers, publishing in *Nature Human Behavior,* were interested in two areas, one of which is endurance during exercise.

For the endurance part, they did genetic testing on the participants to see whether they carried variants of a gene that makes a person prone to tiring easily. In addition, they had people run on a treadmill to measure their endurance. Then, they randomly split the participants into two groups, telling one they had the gene variant that made them tire easily and the other the gene variant that is linked to endurance.

The individuals in the groups, however, were chosen arbitrarily, so some were given accurate results while others were intentionally misled. So, when the participants ran on the treadmill again, their endurance changed measurably-those who were told they had poor endurance genes could not run as long and had poorer lung capacity and more difficulty ridding themselves of carbon dioxide. To the contrary, those who were told they had better endurance ran longer, regardless of what genes they actually carried.

"It's interesting that in the exercise study we saw a negative effect for those who were told they had the high-risk version", Turnwald said in the article. "What was consistent in both studies was that those informed that they had the high-risk gene always had a worse outcome than those informed that they had the protective gene, even though we essentially drew out of a hat which information people received."

Buddhist Monks can meditate for hours on end, abstain from food for days, and execute vows of silence, masterfully exercising control over their bodies more so than the average person. Still, what is particularly amazing is some of them can control physiological functioning such as blood pressure and body temperature-feats many medical doctors find astounding. In one notable exhibit of their skills, a group of monks allowed physicians to monitor their bodily changes as they engaged in a meditative yoga technique (*g Tum-mo*).

During the process, the monks were cloaked in wet, cold sheets (49 f/9.4 c) and placed in a 40 f (4.5 c) room. In such conditions, the average person would likely experience uncontrollable shivering and would shortly suffer hypothermia. However, the monks were able to raise their body heat to generate steam within minutes. Within an hour, the sheets were completely dry. The Buddhists say the heat they generate is a byproduct of the meditation, since it takes energy to reach a state of alternate reality.

In the case of a nocebo effect (a negative expectation), a story was published in the *New Scientist* about a man in Alabama who went to a cemetery and met up with a witch doctor who told him he was going to die soon. Believing in the prediction, he soon fell gravely ill and within a matter of weeks he was close to death. He was taken to the hospital, but the doctors could find nothing wrong with him. After the man's wife told them what happened, one doctor performed a fake procedure on him the next day and he made a full recovery in a short period of time.

Jack Schwarz, a Jewish writer, and Holocaust survivor endured horrific conditions while forced into a Nazi concentration camp during World War II. He was routinely beaten, starved, and tortured beyond imagination. To cope with his situation, he began the practice of meditation and prayer which he developed to the point where he could block out the pain of his torment and subsequently withstand his dire situation.

After his release, Schwarz continued his practice of the mind-body connection and would demonstrate his technique by putting a long sail-maker's needle through his arm without injury. He could also regulate his body's blood flow by causing the puncture hole in his arm to bleed at will. Schwarz was studied by researchers at the Menninger Foundation who found that he indeed learned how to control many of his bodily functions with just his mind.

Dr. Tiller, Professor Emeritus in material science and engineering at Stanford University, conducted experiments to explore whether consciousness or mind power could affect matter. Working with highly trained meditators, Tiller asked them to focus on "imprinting" specific intentions on electrical devices that included water samples. The intent was for the pH of water to go up or down and the samples positively responded exactly as they were intended in the experiment.

Tiller also discovered that over time, his experiments affected the room where they were being conducted, demonstrating even further the power of mind over matter. The object was imparting its qualities to the room so that water placed in the room after the device was removed still affected its pH. He asserted that intention can "change space" so rooms may become "conditioned". In one of his other experiments, intention caused fruit flies to grow 15% faster than normal.

In 2008, at the Cape Fear Valley Medical Center, a hospital in Fayetteville, NC, a woman who appeared to be in her last trimester of pregnancy arrived and was admitted to the maternity ward in preparation for delivery of a child, according to the local ABC affiliate. The woman was seen by resident doctors, and they attempted to induce labor multiple times over the course of two days. After no success, she was scheduled for the ill-fated emergency cesarean procedure, commonly referred to as a c-section.

As she was taken into the operating room, and the surgeon made the incision across her stomach it was discovered that her uterus was empty. She was not pregnant after all. She was suffering from a condition known as pseudocyesis or false pregnancy. Women with this condition can have all the physical signs of pregnancy to include a swollen belly, enlarged breast with milk production, loss of a menstrual cycle, etc., except for an actual fetus. Consequently, two of the doctors were disciplined because of this incident.

According to the doctors at Green & Urribarri, "many women experience the same exact symptoms that a pregnancy would experience. Like mind over matter, your brain can fool your body into thinking that you are pregnant, and therefore, the same exact hormones are released." Dr. Kimberly Gecsi, an obstetrician at University Hospitals in Cleveland said, "most people are convinced they're like 38 weeks along and they come in thinking they're in labor—heavy breathing the whole nine yards", regarding cases of false pregnancies she's experienced over the years.

Another case of unexplained phenomena is when UC-Berkeley professor Elizabeth Lloyd Mayer faced an unfavorable dilemma. One day in 1991, Lisby's 11-year-old daughter Meg's handmade harp was stolen from the theater where she was playing. For two months, Lisby tried everything to recover the harp. The police got involved. She contacted instrument dealers all over the country. A CBS TV news story even aired. But nothing worked. The harp was lost.

Then a friend of Lisby's said, "If you really want that harp back, you should be willing to try anything. Try calling a dowser." Lisby was skeptical. All she knew about dowsers was that they were made up of odd people who walked around with forked sticks telling you where to locate water for drilling wells. But Lisby's friend told her that good dowsers could find not just underground water, but lost objects.

Feeling a sense of desperation, Lisby figured she had nothing to lose. She contacted the president of the American Society of Dowsers, Harold McCoy in Fayetteville, Arkansas, and explained that a harp had been stolen from Oakland, California. She asked Harold if he could help her locate the harp. Harold said, "Give me a second. I'll tell you if it's still in Oakland." He was silent for a moment and then said, "Well, it's still there. Send me a street map of Oakland and I'll locate that harp for you."

Lisby overnighted Harold a map of Oakland. Two days later, he called to give her the address of where the harp was located. Lisby had never heard of the street he named, but she passed the information along to the police. The police shook their heads. They could not issue a search warrant based on a hunch. So Lisby decided to drive over and post flyers within a two-block radius of the address Harold had given her, offering a reward for the return of the harp.

Three days later, her phone rang. A man said that his neighbor had recently showed him the exact harp the flyer was describing. He promised to give it to a teenage boy who would deliver it to her in the rear parking lot of an all-night Safeway grocery store. Despite her own skepticism, Lisby showed up at the appointed time and place, where a young man loaded the harp into the back of her station wagon.

Lisby went on to write a wonderful book "Extraordinary Knowing: Science, Skepticism, and the Inexplicable Powers of the Human Mind", which is full of stories of people who knew things they shouldn't have, as well as the scientific data supporting the existence of paranormal phenomena like telepathy, clairvoyance, remote viewing, and the power of prayer.

The Global Coherence Project, which has existed for nearly 20 years, measures heightened emotions when people around the world are thinking and feeling the same thing. Random Number Generators create sequences of unpredictable ones and zeros. There are currently RGNs in 70 locations around the world. When major events occur, like 9/11 or the deaths of Nelson Mandela or Princess Diana, the numbers stop appearing so random.

At highly eventful and emotional times, the numbers line up amazingly well, breaking the odds of a trillion to one against it happening by chance. They suggest that there is a "noosphere" which responds to people's emotions around the world because of a group consciousness. Though not necessarily a mind over matter study, this experiment reveals a small way of perceiving that human consciousness can have some impact on the physical world.

As humans, we also have a physical attribute that lies dormant for most of our lives and only comes to the surface in extreme situations commonly known as the fight or flight syndrome. This is the body's response to acute stress. The sympathetic nervous system is activated due to the sudden release of hormones. In these moments, people can have superhuman strength and speed that supersedes our physical capabilities. How this process works is not as important as understanding our ability to exceed what we think of as human limitation.

There are documented cases across the country of people who have performed incredible feats that defy logic. Perhaps the most popular story originated in 1962 when Jack Kirby witnessed a woman lift a car off her baby, which inspired him to create the Incredible Hulk, the Marvel comic book character. And in 2006, Lydia Angiyou of Quebec, saved several children by fighting off a polar bear with her bare hands until a local hunter was able to shoot it, but each story shares a common truth about human possibility.

But there are many experiments that serve as evidence of mind over matter. From "intent" that caused a leaf to glow brighter and plants to grow faster to evidence that human consciousness can affect electrical equipment. Human beings are perhaps far more complex and dynamic than what most people realize. We have seen people dance with flames, walk across hot coals, move objects with their minds and heal people with their hands. Perhaps our greatest strength lies in discovering the unknown.

Inspiring Thoughts

Train your mind to see the good in everything. Positivity is a choice. The happiness of your life depends on the quality of your thoughts – Simple Life

You never know how strong you are until being strong is your only choice – Bob Marley

The mind is everything. What you think you become – Buddha

Make your life a masterpiece; imagine no limitations on what you can be, have or do – Brian Tracy

Life is like a camera…focus on what's important. Capture the good times. Develop from the negatives. And if things don't work out, take another shot – author unknown

Everything is energy; your thought begins it; your emotions amplify it and your action increases its momentum – author unknown

You have to grow from the inside out. None can teach you; none can make you spiritual. There is no other teacher but your own soul – Swami Vivekananda

Silence isn't empty, it's full of answers. – author unknown

Miracles start to happen when you give as much energy to your dreams as you do your fears. – author unknown

To be spiritual is not by praying and going to church. Spiritualism is the understanding of the universe so that it can be a better place to live in – Fela Kuti

You are not a human being having a spiritual experience. You are a spiritual being having a human experience – Deepak Chopra

Spirituality is a supreme inter-communication between you and everything – Bryant Gill

If you want to find the secrets of the universe, think in terms of energy, frequency, and vibration – Nikola Tesla

"Every time we have a thought, we make a chemical. If we have good, elevated thoughts or happy thoughts we make chemicals that make us feel good or happy, and if we have negative thoughts or bad thoughts or insecure thoughts, we make chemicals that make us feel exactly the way we are thinking. So, every chemical that it released in the brain is literally a message that feeds the physical body. Now the body begins to feel the way we are thinking". – Joe Dispenza

We are never more than a belief away from our greatest love, deepest healing, and most profound miracles – Dr. Gregg Braden

"Quantum healing is healing the body/mind from a quantum level. That means from a level which is not manifest at a sensory level. Our bodies ultimately are fields of information, intelligence and energy. Quantum healing involves a shift in the fields of energy information, so as to bring about a correction in an idea that has gone wrong. So, quantum healing involves healing one mode of consciousness, mind, to bring about changes in another mode of consciousness, body." – Dr. Deepak Chopra

Your positive action combined with positive thinking results in success – Shiv Khera

Create the highest, grandest vision possible for your life, because you become what you believe – author unknown

Positive thinking is more than just a tagline, it changes the way we behave. And I firmly believe that when I am positive, it not only makes me better, but it also makes those around me better- Harvey Mackey

There are two ways of spreading light: to be the candle or the mirror that reflects it- Edith Wharton

Only in the darkness can you see the stars- Dr. Martin Luther King, Jr.

There are no limits to what you can accomplish, except the limits you place on your own thinking- Brian Tracy

If you realized how powerful your thoughts are, you would never think a negative thought again - Natural Life

What consumes your mind, controls your life – author unknown

We can complain because rose bushes have thorns or rejoice because thorns have roses – Alphonse Kerr

Attract what you expect, reflect what you desire, become what you respect, mirror what you admire – author unknown

The Red Pill

In the movie, The Matrix, the character Neo is offered the choice between a red pill and a blue pill. The red pill represents an uncertain future, but it would free him from the dominating control of the dream world. The blue pill represents an attractive prison of confined comfort and blissful ignorance. As it is put by Morpheus: "You take the blue pill…the story ends, you wake up in your bed and believe whatever it is you want to believe. You take the red pill…you stay in wonderland, and I show you how deep the rabbit hole goes".

There is a documented story of a woman named Yvonne who worked at a supermarket stocking shelves when she was accidently sprayed in the face with window cleaner and lost her vision. Feeling burning in both eyes, she was taken to the hospital where her eyes were examined and washed. Given the all-clear, she was released to go home. But the next morning, her vision was blurring, and it continued to deteriorate throughout the day. When she opens her eyes the next morning, she was completely blind.

Over the next six months, Yvonne underwent several tests, but nothing could be found to be wrong with her. Yet she could not see. Yvonne was referred to Suzanne O'Sullivan for a neurological examination. Dr. O'Sullivan recalls gathering around her bed with a group of junior doctors and medical students as a series of eye examinations were carried out. She, along with everyone else present, became skeptical when Yvonne reacted to tests as a person with normal vision would.

Her eyes involuntarily responded to the rotating drum of alternating black and white stripes being spun in front of her, for instance, and blinked when a consultant lifted an ophthalmoscope to her eye. After a couple of more weeks of tests, which showed that the integrity of Yvonne's visual pathway was intact and there was not any neurological damage to explain her loss of vision, the explanation was "functional" blindness caused by stress.

This news did not go over so well as Yvonne and her family were displeased with the doctor's diagnosis and disputed her conclusion. Nevertheless, she agreed to see a psychiatrist-if only as her husband put it, to prove the doctors wrong. However, they were correct. After six months of psychiatric treatment, Yvonne's vision returned to normal. Yvonne is one of many people who have convinced themselves they are blind, unable to move arms or legs, who suffer from pain and fatigue- for no biological reason.

"It's All in Your Head: True Stories of Imaginary Illness" is a book by Dr. Suzanne O'Sullivan which gives account of patients she's treated over 20 years as a consultant neurologist at the National Hospital of Neurology and Neurosurgery in London. In her book, she argues for a more compassionate understanding of mind related illnesses and leaves little doubt that her patients are suffering from real symptoms.

The mind-body conundrum has been the subject of medical, psychological, philosophical, and religious inquiry for centuries. However, it has long been known that they are connected even if it is unclear as to how or to what extent. It has been noted that he placebo effect is so strong that it must be accounted for in most clinical drug trials; for many conditions the real drug is often only marginally better than the fake one, especially for those aimed at problems that have a strong subjective element, such as pain, mood and sleep. Drug effects have as much to do with expectation as pharmaceutical properties.

According to O'Sullivan, suggesting to someone they may have thought themselves sick is often interpreted, and quite often intended, as a rebuke. She stated "When people with diabetes or asthma are stressed and their diabetes goes out of control or their asthma gets worse, people can accept that because there's an actual disease at the heart of it. But this idea that you can think yourself sick is almost like a personal insult. People see it as a judgement of their personalities".

Yet, along with the placebo effect there is also the nocebo effect. People given an inert drug which they believe has adverse side effects will often report the symptoms they believe to be associated with the drug. While they may be mostly subjective symptoms, such as nausea or pain, they occasionally show up as rashes, skin problems and other symptoms that are sometimes detectable on physiological tests.

As an example, Dr. O'Sullivan pointed to the condition called koro, which is most common among Asian men who become convinced their penis is shrinking and will go to the hospital with it grasped in their hand to prevent it from retracting into their bodies. In the 1990s, when Western media gave a lot of attention to an apparent candida (yeast) epidemic, doctors saw numerous women convinced their symptoms (tiredness, irritable, craving sugar) could be a result of it.

In the 2016 article, Mind Over Matter by Margo White, "Psychosomatic conditions have been with us forever, and the interesting thing about them is the fact they change shape and nature depending on what is current in the zeitgeist," stated Keith Petrie, professor of psychological medicine at the

University of Auckland. He further added "stress has become an established issue people blame illness for, so illnesses take on that sort of shape. At the moment, we're in an environment where concerns about food are prominent…and we're getting a lot of food-related allergies and gluten intolerance."

When Dr. O'Sullivan first started practicing as a neurologist, she stated that one of the most common problems she saw was what is generally referred to in neurological circles as dissociative seizures, sometimes called non-epileptic seizures, functional seizures, psychogenic seizures or pseudo-seizures. She espoused that these attacks look very similar to epilepsy but are not caused by disrupted electrical activity. Instead, they are linked to mental and emotional processes-the body's involuntary reaction to difficult thoughts and feelings.

According to O'Sullivan, in an average neurology clinic, one in three people has a functional neurological disorder, and in an epilepsy clinic, one in five has dissociative seizures. She laments that she was constantly telling people about this diagnosis, aware of how common it is, but every time she told someone, they were shocked. They had never heard of it. But it is not obscure or something that only happens to a small number of people. But this goes to show how much of a neglected area it is, and how ill-informed society is about what is an ordinary problem.

According to experts, there are numerous mechanisms involved in psychosomatic illnesses. Dissociative seizures can be but are not always linked with loss, grief, or abuse. People with unexplained muscle spasms or paralysis may be more informed by a past injury, their expectations of recovery and by paying too much attention to their own symptoms, exacerbating them to the point of debilitation as sometimes the mind can be too active.

In the same article it was noted that Dr. Brian Broom of the immunology department at Auckland City Hospital, does not see a separation in the mind-body connection and advocates what he calls a "whole person" approach to treatment. This stance dismisses the dualistic mind/body model upon which contemporary medicine, he argues, rests; especially since the 20th century, as advances in the understanding of biological disease and developing technologies have made it easier to measure, investigate and detect physical abnormalities.

According to Broom, the "whole person" approach "lets in not just mind, but family, relationships, employment, social networks, culture, spirituality, when appropriate. It gives permission to consider the whole person, rather than the old framework of mind or body, psychosomatic or organic." "And then the doctor might ask, 'What was the most interesting, memorable, worrying, hard thing that was happening to you when it started- or, more recently, when you had a flare-up.'"

Oftentimes, when something occurs in the body it is not uncommon for something to be going on in your life that either coincides with it or acts as a precursor to it. Sometimes a physical condition is brought on by the perception of a lifechanging event. "One woman", said Broom, suffered from urticaria. After she was told it could be related to a personal experience, "the woman went away, thought about it, came back, talked about it and in a few weeks, the urticaria went away."

Karen Lindsay who works as an immunologist and rheumatologist, adopted her wholistic method of treatment from Broom. She went through medical school and learned the right language, the anatomy, the physiology, and pharmacology, but had a feeling she was missing something. She had a patient who had anaphylaxis with fish after his boat blew up and a woman who, on the day she was made bankrupt, had an anaphylaxis to mussels for the first time. Lindsay stated that when patients are alerted to a possible link between what is going on in their life and what is going on in their body, they often get better.

The Matrix movie depicts a dystopian future in which humanity is unknowingly trapped inside a simulated reality, created by intelligent machines to distract humans while using their bodies as an energy source. When the character Neo discovers the truth, he is drawn into rebellion against machines along with other people who have been freed from the Matrix. Which pill are you going to choose, the blue or the red?

Innergy vs. Religion

People who are unfamiliar with consciousness or mind over matter often confuse the concept with some form of religion or theocracy in general. Instead of understanding innergy (internal energy) as a separate entity or body of work they attempt to place it in a religious context to explain it from a theological perspective. In doing so, it undermines the field of study and marginalizes its value while simultaneously giving greater credit, recognition, and viable substance to a religious methodology.

Innergy is not religion. In fact, innergy is an act of spirituality in meaning that it is a natural and organic exercise of human activity that centers on our thoughts and feelings. It does not require a doctrine because the lessons are taught by life experiences. There are no formal directives to speak of because the very nature of the act reveals the benefits of positivity, rightness, truth, balance, and reciprocity. It is an unspoken and active adherence to divine communication between the conscious mind and the field.

On the other hand, religion is an organized belief system. It requires that people follow a certain protocol in terms of how they exercise faith in accordance with the progenitors and leaders of the practice. In general, religion postulates that humans are powerless and oblivious without conviction and are prone to self-destructive habits and behaviors without religious guidance, leadership, and moral parameters. So, there is a sense of dependency on the part of followers who concede control over their lives to a religious institution.

The idea that humans believe we have a god all to ourselves, an almighty supreme being who created us in his/her own image, is quite disturbing from a psychological point of view. To believe the earth and everything within it was made for our special benefit suggests that we as people are extremely narcissistic. We see ourselves as a superior species based on the idea of higher intelligence despite the fact the we are the most destructive creatures on the planet. There is no social problem that exist that humans did not create. There is no environmental problem that exist that we did not create.

Over time we have committed the most heinous crimes against humanity to include slavery, war, colonialism, holocaust, and genocide. We have subjected human beings to cruel, inhumane, and harsh treatments of torture from medical experiments and concentration camps to lynching. We have forcefully removed animals from their natural habitats for nothing more than our own personal gains of pleasure and profits while we kill them for sport and leisure. We have contaminated the ocean waters all around the world with our trash and tons of plastic and burned a hole in the ozone layer because of our chemicals and pollutants. Each year humans kill each other by the thousands and yet we think we have a god.

Religions have been responsible for some of the worst atrocities throughout the ages. You cannot talk about Hinduism without mentioning its' shameful and bigoted history of the caste system.   You cannot talk about Islam without discussing jihad and the Bagt Treaty regarding the invasions and enslavement of the Sudanese people. And you certainly can't talk about Christianity without discussing the inhumane and horrific experience of the transatlantic slave trade and over three hundred years of incomprehensible suffering from human captivity, and to a lesser extent, the role Judaism played in support of it.

This is not to say a higher power does not exist just perhaps not in a religious context. Rhonda Byrnes authored the popular book titled "The Secret" several years ago and since then other writers have penned similar works which has made the phrase "law of attraction" socially acceptable. The law of attraction is what we refer to when we talk about innergy. However, the fundamental difference is when they speak on it as if it is a magnetic process, the concept doesn't go any further. It stops right there as if it is self-explanatory.

But if Jack and Jane live 10 miles apart and they each share the same desire, how do they come together to meet? In other words, if you order a package it doesn't just instantly appear at your doorstep. It requires a courier service to transport it from point A to point B. If there is nothing in the air but empty space, then our thoughts would go no further than our own minds. So, there must be something that exist for an attraction to materialize and the something that I am speaking on is the field.

When we talk about the field, it is in the context of a supreme or godlike presence and power, but it is literally in the air we breathe. It is more of an invisible matter as opposed to a man or a woman sitting above the clouds. It does not have a physical body, name or scriptures, prophets, saints, or saviors but it is an intelligent, unseen substance of energy that surrounds us. It exists as the clear, open space between people and physical objects that we were taught to perceive as "nothing". It has no beginning or end, but it is the source that connects to our consciousness and powers everything in the world.

Here is an example of how it works. In the early 1990s, Richard Geggie went to see his doctor because he continuously felt tired and listless. He was sent to have an electrocardiogram. Later that day, when the results came back, he was told that his heart was at serious risk. He was instructed to stay calm, not exert himself, keep nitroglycerine pills with him, and not to go outside alone. The doctors administered several tests over the following days, and he failed them all because his arteries were severely clogged.

Tests included an angiogram, electrocardiogram, and a stress test. As a high-risk patient, he was given an immediate appointment for heart bypass surgery. The day before the surgery, he surprisingly woke up feeling better. He went to the hospital and was given an angiogram. This involved shooting dye into his arteries through an injection in his thigh. His chest was shaved as he awaited surgery when the new angiogram results returned from the lab.

The doctor in charge looked at them and became visibly upset and said he had wasted his time. There were no blockages visible at all. He could not explain why all the initial tests revealed severe problems. Unbeknownst to Richard, a friend in California, a Pomo Indian medicine man, assembled a group of his students upon hearing of his heart condition, and performed a healing ceremony the day before his second angiogram. The next day he was healed.

According to Gregg Braden, a New Age author who links science and spirituality, "When we have a feeling in our hearts, we are creating electric and magnetic waves that extend beyond our bodies into the world around us. And what's interesting is the research that shows those waves extend not just one or two meters beyond where our hearts reside but many kilometers away from where our physical hearts are."

We each carry an aura of our conscious mind around us every day which is very much like a spotlight. This is how you can walk into a room and instantly feel a level of comfort or uneasiness because you are picking up on the vibe of the environment. It is how you can meet people for the very first time and feel as if you have known them all your life. Some people seem to click, hit it off for no apparent reason and this happens before they learn of anything they have in common.

There is a sense of intuition as well. It is the sensation you get when you can feel someone is staring at you from a distance. It also happens when people experience fear, and you can feel the hair raise up on the back of your neck and arms. I've always had a lukewarm relationship with dogs since I was a child growing up and not too long ago, I was driving to my aunt's house who hadn't had a dog since her "Ginger" passed away in over a decade.

As soon as I turned the corner about a mile away, it hit me that she had a dog at her house. I do not know how or why but I was prepared as soon I pulled into her driveway. When her stepdaughter opened the garage, immediately a black and white Boston terrier, "Diamond", darted out towards us, running in circles and jumping around uncontrollably. I was already studying innergy at the time, but I could not stop thinking about how amazing this revelation was.

There is a popular experiment on the power of thought that has since been repeated several times over the years using two jars of cooked rice. On the outside of one jar the word love was written and on the front of the other jar was the word hate. For the next few weeks everyone who participated in the experiment walked past the love jar and expressed positive, complimentary words and sentiments towards it.

When they came across the hate jar, they did the exact opposite by spouting hateful, incendiary, and angry words and thoughts in its direction. At the end of the experiment it was clear that both containers of rice absorbed the energy they received. The rice in the love jar remained white with a fresh appearance while the rice in the hate jar had rotted and turned discolored. Each jar reflected the thoughts and attitudes it was exposed to from the external environment.

IKEA, the furniture super store, conducted its own experiment on bullying by using two plants from its store. With the help of the Wellington Academy school in Dubai, students walked past the two plants, complimenting and encouraging one in a pleasant voice while verbally assaulting the other with hateful words in an angry tone for one month, and the results were the same as with the rice. The plant receiving the positive messages blossomed while the other one wilted.

In general, if the field is what transmits our thoughts, and there seems to be no limitation in terms of space, time and distance, then we can assume it's the same source of energy that allows the world to function in an organized and orderly manner. We know a presence of energy is evident all around us because a source sustains all forms of life to include everything in nature. Whether it glows or grows, it requires energy.

This is the power that rotates the planet in a steady motion that we call time. The field is what maintains the necessities of life and the elements of earth with the rain, sun, wind and light to produce the greenery of nature, the beautiful blue waves of the ocean and the majestic ridges and valleys of the mountains. It is the energy that illuminates the sky at night and gives the earth a bold and colorful view from every corner of the globe.

It is the presence of the field that we must recognize and revere. It is our thoughts that we must continue to shape, mold, chisel and hone into positive viewpoints and perspectives. This requires a greater capacity of understanding, insight, and wisdom in our service of humanity allowing us to establish respect, dignity, and honor in our lives and in our relationships with others. This is the most sacred and valuable lesson we can learn from the field; to think and feel peace, love and harmony is to create it.

How to Create the Life You Want

How to create the life you want is relatively simple in application. Discipline, however, is our greatest challenge. Whatever thought you have in your conscious mind is what you will manifest. It is the thought that you give your focus and attention to that will be a part of your reality and it must be sincere to have the emotional thread that it requires. This is what we call internal energy.

When we talk about a conscious thought, we are referring to what you believe to be of extreme importance. You may know the words to your favorite song and can sing along to the tune but it's not a conscious thought in the same way that you might pray on behalf of a loved one who is sick. It is one thing to want something but something completely different when you feel as though you need it.

This process is commonly referred to as the law of attraction. But there are two parts to everything in life and before we talk about the law of attraction, we must understand the law of duality. Your thought is one part of the process but what happens on the other side of your thought? A thought emits energy out into the universe which is what we call the field. The field creates the screen play that an entire cast of people unknowingly act out in the real world to complete your conscious thought.

There are volumes of scientific evidence to prove that our thoughts alone have immediate and tangible effects on our lives and the environment around us. For example, in the summer of 1993, a meditation experiment was conducted in Washington, DC. A group of 4,000 people participated in meditating on peace and love to reduce criminal activity in high-crime areas of the city. A team of scientists and researchers tested for every variable imaginable and the results were striking. During the month of meditation, crime dropped by 25%.

Take for example the odds of winning a lottery jackpot. According to Lottery USA, the odds of winning the Mega Millions jackpot are 1 in 302.6 million and the odds of winning the Powerball are 1 in 292.2 million. The chances of winning are pretty much the same as being struck by lightning. Therefore, how do we account for people who hit big lottery prizes more than once?

A woman in Durham, North Carolina did just that. In 2018, she won $4 million dollars and won $1 million dollars two years later. In Ohio, a resident won huge jackpots twice in 5 months. In Indianapolis, Robert Hamilton won $1 million dollars on two separate occasions in a span of three months.

Calvin and Zatera Spencer won two $ 1 million-dollar prizes, a $50,000 and a $100,000 prize in the same year. Joan Ginther won 4 times for a total of more than $20 million dollars. In Missouri, Ernest Pullen won $1 million dollars and a year later hit again for $2 million. Melvyn Wilson, Rolf Rhodes, and Valerie Wilson each have multiple wins for millions of dollars because a conscious mindset does not recognize "mathematical odds."

But the field itself is neutral. It is equally balanced. It reflects your intent no matter what it is you believe. If you espouse hate the field will provide you a platform. If you are an advocate for justice, the field will grant you a voice in law and order. It is the mirror that will only reflect what you put in front of it, whether it is good, bad, right, wrong, or indifferent. The lessons you learn from the results, however, is what postulates positivity over negativity when we apply knowledge, wisdom and understanding.

Therefore, we must be careful of our thoughts. What we allow ourselves to think can have a profound impact on our lives to include severe consequences. We must equally be cautious of what and who we allow to influence our thinking. What is the message in the music that you listen to? What acts are portrayed on the television shows and movies you watch? What is the nature of the conversations you have with the people you associate with? Because everything you engage in affects what you think and believe which in turn creates the world around you.

One of the problems people often deal with when it comes to the law of attraction is, they have several things they want all at once: money, love, friendships, career, opportunities, etc. Therefore, they put a casual amount of energy into each area instead of zeroing in on one at a time with laser sharp focus. It is the same as if someone were to diet and exercise one day versus five days a week, the results are going to be equivalent to the effort.

I have a cousin who tragically died a little more than 13 years ago. One night recently I woke up at one o'clock in the morning thinking about him before eventually going back to sleep. I never shared this with my wife but by the time we were up to start the day, she invited me to join her for an early morning walk in the neighborhood.

As soon as we strolled a couple of blocks from the house, my wife made a statement and accidently mentioned my cousin by name. I never responded to her gaffe, but I smiled and shook my head in wonderment as she continued talking. This is to say the energetic vibrations from your conscious thoughts surround you like an aura that others pick up on.

It is also important to understand that there are seven billion people on the planet. Everyone has a conscious mindset and they are exercising energy for their own benefit. This means that we potentially navigate through clusters of energy every day because the mechanic needs someone's car to break down. The dentist needs someone who requires an extraction, the plumber needs someone to have a water leak, etc. So, at times we have all succumbed to the energy of other people under given circumstances.

In psychology, there is the internal vs. external locus of control. This essentially means, do you believe you can influence your environment, so things happen for you or do you believe things only happen to you? As we have demonstrated in several examples, the answer can be both. However, you have the power to maintain control of your own life when you live a life of purpose and intent. It leaves little room for you to participate in someone else's script.

Once you apply the techniques of consciousness, you will begin to see immediate changes in your life. You will be able to attract money whether it comes in the form of a new job, an unexpected check, a crisp bill in front of your feet or a significant savings from an expense that goes away. Focus on love and you will come across a new attraction. The same methodology applies to your health, career, and all other aspects of life.

The possibilities are boundless, but the first step is to believe that it actually works. You cannot say to the field 'this is what I want' or 'this is what I need'. The field will only respond to your conscious thought and intention. Real thought, real intent, real emotions. Anything else is not going to work. If I say, there is a six-digit code to unlock a bank vault you cannot spin any six numbers and expect the door to open. It must be the correct set of numbers for the combination to work.

If you want to test the waters and start out with something small to build your belief and confidence, I would say to think of an old friend, or a deceased relative who may have passed away some years ago. In either case, it should be someone you were close to and then spend a few days reminiscing on the fond memories the two of you shared. Then casually engage in conversations with family members and friends without mentioning anything about the person you thought about and see if their name or anything related to them comes up by chance.

There are other tests that can be done on a small scale as well. Something simple as finding a parking space or a random $10.00 on the ground. Thinking about a co-worker you have not spoken to for some time is another possibility, but these ideas fall into somewhat of a gray area. The main reason is because there is no real emotional attachment to finding money on the ground or parking a car at the supermarket. This is not to say they cannot work but I would advise to start with something that involves true feelings.

If it is something you are going to pray about, remember that it starts in the conscious mind. It is the nature of the thought itself before it is spoken. The essence of spiritual communication is not in words but in the energy our thoughts emit into the Universe. In other words, a child does not have to understand a parent's frustration because it is recognized in the tone of their voice. This essentially means that prayer is a non-verbal language which is the true essence of a spiritual expression.

Practice unconditional love. This is paramount so that you feel deserving of what you are asking for. Your deep subconscious fears and doubts send messages loud and clear that interferes with your positive focus. If a part of you feels undeserving of what you are seeking, then that becomes a belief in and of itself that conflicts with what you desire. It is like the static between two radio stations competing for a signal and neither one comes through very clearly. Therefore, know your frequency and stay on it. Believe all things are possible.

Mindfulness is paying attention to the present moment. It is an act of conscious awareness. When you are mindful you are not thinking about the past or what might happen in the future. Your focus is on the here and now. Practicing mindfulness is a way of training yourself to become aware of thought patterns without judging them as good or bad, right, or wrong. It can also lead to less stress and depression while improving sleep and overall wellbeing.

Studies have shown that practicing mindful meditation, even for short periods, have improved the ability to focus, make decisions, and manage emotions. The key is to pay attention to the present moment. Take breaks throughout the day to simply focus on what is going on in the present moment. Notice the air, warm or cool, the sound of noise or quietness, the sensations you feel in your body, or your thoughts and feelings. Scan your body to pick up on any sensations or feelings, starting with your feet and move up to your head.

Notice any place that might feel tense or tight and attempt to address it by reversing the feeling by means of imagination. Focus on breathing. When you feel stress or anxiety, close your eyes, and breathe in deeply and count to four. Count to eight as you exhale, which triggers your body to relax. Observe and address your thoughts, then ask yourself is it a thought of worry, and if so, let it go. Practice these techniques on a regular basis and the more you do, the better you will become.

Emotional fitness is when you can maintain a positive outlook in any given situation. It means facing and overcoming challenges and problem solving with a can-do attitude. Positive thinking is being able to see the best in yourself and others. It means to feed your subconscious mind with positive mantras throughout the day, words and music that produces positive thoughts. It means to set and pursue short and long-term goals, small increments of success to build upon.

What can equally be disruptive in exercising innergy is your relationship with others. Most of us underestimate the innergy of other people but we must be careful and aware of our associations. Disagreements, arguments, and conflicts on any level can lead to negative energy against you. Negative thoughts towards you can lead to disarray in your life and constant turmoil. Remember, their innergy is just as powerful towards you as yours is in attracting what you desire.

Be open minded and respectful when you interact with others. Do not come across as judgmental and critical but practice kindness and understanding even if you do not necessarily agree with them on all matters. You must stay humble and mindful to keep some thoughts to yourself if you feel they may be offensive, misconstrued or misinterpreted by someone else.

Maintain peace, harmony, and goodwill because the absence of negative innergy clears the path for good things to come.

Experience the reality of what you desire. Have a clear and vivid imagination of what you want in your mind. Repeat this image several times a day throughout the day and weeks ahead so that it becomes a conscious thought. Once your conscious thought becomes the aura that surrounds you, the field will put the plan in motion and design how, when and where it all happens. If you remain focused, it is just a matter of time before you see the results.

A Message to Black Lives Matter

In 1997, a black man named Ferris Shelton wrote an article in
Emerge magazine about his nightmarish account of being pulled
over by a white police officer. He said the event occurred early
on Thanksgiving morning. He and his family packed into their
minivan and drove from Springfield, Massachusetts and were on
their way to Virginia Beach, Va., when they were stopped en
route by law enforcement.

They were on the highway in Maryland when he looked up and
saw the blue flashing lights, then he checked the speedometer
and realized he was driving close to 80 miles an hour.
Apparently, the last time he checked the highway speed limit it
was 70 mph, but he was now traveling in a different zone.
While he was being pulled over, he stated that he could feel an
"unrecognizable and yet somehow familiar fear" that began
inside of him.

But the fear growing in him was not based on getting a speeding
ticket. He described it as a gripping fear that was predicated on
something else altogether. He did not know what it was but
that "something else" commanded his full attention. As he
began applying his brakes, the first of many thoughts came to
mind. Did he have anything in the van that could cause a
problem; no weapons, stolen items, alcohol, or drugs, as he
went down the checklist.

He glanced in the rearview mirror and saw that his kids were
asleep along with his wife in the passenger seat. He woke up
his wife and said, "Honey, we have a problem." He then began
rehearsing his responses to the state trooper. His hope of
having a Black patrolman was soon dashed as the trooper's car

rolled through the light and he could see in his mirror that the officer was a White male.

His level of anxiety rose as he wondered how he was going to be perceived by the officer. Was he going to be matched to a stereotypical image of a Black male with criminal tendencies and a proclivity to violence? Was he too articulate, which might offend the officer as he may be perceived as an "uppity n-word"? He suddenly had visions of Rodney King's video in mind as he wondered if he would be victimized in similar fashion.

In the end, however he drove away with a $150.00 speeding ticket. His exchange with the officer was uneventful but imagine what it's like to be gripped with perpetual fear each time you encounter an officer and asking yourself "what if"? He concluded that his concerns were "unrealized but not unfounded". They were grounded in the fact that as African Americans, we are potentially at risk whenever we encounter White police officers.

One of my earliest run-ins with law enforcement occurred when I was just a student in college in Fayetteville, North Carolina. My brother and I were walking home from class when we were stopped in the middle of a neighborhood street by a White officer who asked to look inside of our book bags. I was 19 at the time and didn't really understand the gravity of the situation but it bothered me for a long time and I never forgot the humiliating experience.

From that moment on, society made it clear to me that I was a Black man first and everything else about me was secondary to my race. I can recall walking in stores and being followed by security because I was being suspected of shoplifting before I had the opportunity to make a purchase. As an adult, I was passed over on two jobs for less qualified White men.

I was pulled over by police 14 times in a matter of five years for "driving while black" and never received a ticket for an infraction. I don't have a criminal record to speak of, I don't drink, smoke and I've never used or sold drugs. I was not driving a BMW or a Cadillac Escalade but a used Chevy Corsica and a 20-year-old Volkswagen Rabbit.

As I was growing up, my parents use to take me and my brothers with them to visit with family in their hometown of North Carolina. There was a sign at the entrance that said, "The Ku Klux Klan welcomes you to Smithfield" with a picture of a Klansman on a horse. This sign was a stark warning to Blacks but had a different connotation for Whites. For us, it was in no uncertain terms to 'stay in your place or else' and for them it was a red carpet being rolled out that underscored white privilege and the open acceptance of bigotry.

But my personal experiences are the common experiences of most Black people in America. And this did not happen to me in the 40s, 50s or 60s but it started in the 1980s and continued into the 2000s. It happened during the time the world witnessed Rodney King being beaten by white police officers on a grainy video. He laid on the ground motionless while they continued swinging their billy clubs battering his listless body. It was also during the time of the Central Park five, Amadou Diallo, James Byrd Jr, and many others who have been victimized by racism in America.

To the members of BLM, I must say that I am pleasantly surprised at how many of our young people are actively engaged in struggle. You are courageously marching and protesting in cities across America, primarily as a reaction to the untimely and unjustly death of George Floyd but also for the many others who were brutally murdered by the hands of police officers.

Along with your passion and bravery is a hint of naivete. You are fearless considering the number of Black people who have been killed or imprisoned for taking a stand against injustice with the likes of Medgar Evers, Geronimo Pratt and others who marched and fought for our rights as a people. Perhaps fear would have compromised the necessary arrogance of standing face to face with armed officers who typically see us as less than human.

Abner Louima was being treated at a Coney Island Hospital after being brutally beaten and sodomized in the restroom of a New York City police station. When his family tried to file a complaint against the officer involved, they were laughed at and met with snide, condescending remarks as they were escorted out the door. However, this is indicative of how we have been treated by law enforcement ever since the "overseer" became the "officer".

We are reminded of the Declaration of Independence that includes the words "liberty" and "equality", but it did not prevent states from enacting slave codes that imposed brutal control over Black people. In fact, the nation quantified Black inferiority as three-fifths of a human being. What were the remaining percentages other than to say that were viewed as part animal? There was nothing written that kept the Supreme Court from holding in the Dred Scott case that slaves weren't citizens and observing that they had, at the time of the founding of the Republic, "no rights which the White man was bound to respect."

Therefore, I am immensely proud of every one of you who have stepped up for justice. You have taken our cause and put it in the face of America and said in no uncertain terms that change is going to happen, not tomorrow, not next year, but right now! Our mistreatment is not going to be tolerated or accepted. We are going to make a difference by any means necessary.

For nearly nine minutes, George Floyd's neck was pinned under the knee of a white Minneapolis police officer, which resulted in his death. Eric Garner died from a police chokehold after repeatedly being heard saying "I can't breathe". Breonna Taylor, Ahmaud Arbery, and the list goes on and on. So, our fight is a fight for justice, dignity, and respect so that we are recognized as human beings and our lives have as much value as everyone else's.

It comes as no surprise that in June of 2020, three white police officers in North Carolina were heard on tape having what they thought was a private conversation. At the 46-minute mark of the video, Officers Piner and Gilmore began talking from their respective cars, at which time Piner criticized the department, saying its only concern was "kneeling down with the black folks."

About 30 minutes later, Piner received a phone call from Moore in which Moore used a racial epithet (the n-word) to refer to a Black woman. He repeated the use of the slur in describing a Black magistrate as well. Later in the conversation, according to the investigation, Piner told Moore that he feels a civil war is coming and that he Is ready. Piner said he was going to buy a new assault rifle, and soon "we are just going to go out and start slaughtering them (expletive) Blacks." "I can't wait. God, I can't wait."

Understand the mentality of what we are dealing with. It is important that we focus on police brutality and murder at the hands of law enforcement but let us not lose sight of White supremist organizations and militias and their plans to exterminate the Black race. We must equally be aware of redlining, housing discrimination and gerrymandering because racism is wide ranging and our focus on it must be as well. It all falls under the same umbrella of hate.

But BLM is a continuation of the Black power movement of the 1960s and 70s. This is when the Black Panthers, US, SNCC, the civil rights movement and the Nation of Islam addressed the myriad of issues affecting the Black community. They built the platform that Black Lives Matter stand on today.

Thank you for your service and let us continue to fight until there is nothing left to fight for!

Where Do We Go from Here?

A little more than 20 years ago, I crafted and developed a concept that I call a cultural orientation. After extensive reading and conducting research on the Black experience in America and abroad, it occurred to me that everything is rooted in culture. Every race has a language, education, religion, names, and customs that comes from their historical past and the exclusive commonalities are what binds them together as a people.

This idea was conceived early on during my formative years of what is typically referred to as coming into knowledge of self. It started with reading the Autobiography of Malcolm X and the book literally shook my soul to the core. My ignorance of not understanding who I was as a Black man of African descent began to unravel like a peel around an onion.

I was the deacon in my church at the time and I could feel the sting of Malcom's words as he talked about the White man's Christian religion and how it was used to justify our enslavement. It may not have been the message I wanted to hear but it's the one that I needed because I was walking around in ignorant bliss like most African Americans who have never been consciously awakened.

My life was rapidly changing at this point and I could not stop reading. I read about four or five books on Malcolm in the following months and began purchasing video and cassette tapes of his interviews and live speeches. In realizing that I was limited in my understanding of the Black experience, I began reading dozens of books from "Soul on Ice" by Eldridge Cleaver and "From the Browder Files" by Tony Browder to "The Rage of A Privilege Class" by Ellis Cose.

I began purchasing copies of the Final Call newspaper and subscribing to Emerge Magazine. It was an exciting time for me in terms of personal growth because my mind was like a caterpillar in the process of becoming a butterfly. However, I quickly realized that there is a wealth of information on the Black experience coming from various perspectives that were not always complementary.

There were sources coming from religious sects, educators, politicians, journalists, activists, and others so I decided to narrow my focus on the African-centered school of thought. In doing so, I was able to understand the Pan African movement, how it addressed systemic and global racism and emphasized culture as a primary means of empowerment.

I began to read the works of scholars such as Clarke, Ben and Diop. Their books are the monumental works on the African American experience and throughout the diaspora. They were teaching as professors in major universities in America and abroad and were featured on national television and in the mainstream news media. They were leading study tours in Egypt to show the evidence of its' African origins and other expeditions across the continent. In other words, they were fighting our battles on the frontline.

They provided key information on the Black experience from ancient Kemet and the Moors to Garveyism. They spoke about the Black power movements and inner-city struggles and they debated European scholars along the way. But there were two books that stood out from the rest and influenced my concept of a cultural orientation: Afrocentricity by Dr. Molefi Kete Asante and the Kwanzaa holiday by Dr. Maulana Karenga.

These two books speak on the dynamics of culture, its purpose and power. They are clear in the fact that everything is rooted in culture: religion, art, names, history, language, food, activities, beliefs, education, customs, etc. That culture is the grounding for all people around the world and the continuity of passing on traditions from one generation to the next is how people maintain their historical prominence.

But for African Americans, one of the main strategies of slavery was to decimate African culture. So, they stripped us of our language, education, religion, names and customs and they were replaced with the cultural elements of White America. In the process, we were taught to hate Africa and to be ashamed of our African features as we began to view the world from the cultural lens of our oppressors. In doing so, we became disengaged from each other and disconnected from our historical roots.

Without the commonalities of culture, we began to see each other as essentially strangers in a strange land. Perhaps it was a brilliant chess move on the part of the slave master because it prevented us from uniting in great numbers. They made sure we had nothing in common aside from our complexion and collective suffering which was grounded in fear. Ultimately, it lessened the threat and effectiveness of slave rebellions and revolts as it does in our ability to empower our communities today.

Most African Americans are unaware of what it means to be culturally conscious. Therefore, I devised the principles of an orientation to simplify it so that it can be understood in layman terms by the masses of our people. This is to say that if we only engage in White America's elements of cultural then it is impossible for us to have knowledge of ourselves when we're a people of African descent.

Simply put, if there is no identifiable Africaness in us, we are not only culturally deficient, but we are incapable of having substantive dialog on matters of race as it pertains to freedom, justice, and equality. It is impossible if we are using someone else's cultural framework to define who we are. Any position we take is compromised. And yet, how do we engage in our own orientation if our allegiance is with the cultural elements of another people?

I began to see a correlation between the suffering in our community and our lack of an orientation which culminates in our inability to work together in unison. We have a disproportionate amount of poverty, disease, addiction, crime, imprisonment, unemployment, homelessness, and single-parent households. The fact that we are the only people without culture may explain why we have so many social, political, and economic problems.

So, I began to ask the question how does culture work and why is it effective? To answer this question, it was necessary to study other communities that are steep in culture. Jews, for example, are one of the richest and well-developed ethic groups in America. They have their own established communities where they own, operate and control most of their economy, jobs, education, religion, and politics.

When we speak of a Jewish community, we can start with their orientation. First, they speak the English language and are typically well versed in Hebrew and Yiddish. Their education includes the history and the reestablishing of the state of Israel, Auschwitz and the experience of the holocaust, the story of

Abram and their unique contributions to the world. Their primary religion is Judaism, they have typical Jewish names and engage in customs such as Hanukkah, Rosh Hashanah, Yom Kippur, and Bar Mitzvah.

As a result of their internal commonalities, they have close-knit communities which highlights the effectiveness of their orientation. Their social grounding creates a synergy that allows the members of their community to work and build together and to trust and respect each other. It enables them to form a network of cooperative economics which allows the storekeeper, barber, and restaurateur to patronize each other's business to circulate their money and generate community wealth.

You see a similar scenario with the Chinese as they have established a Chinatown in every major city in America. And what did they bring with them when they came over to the U.S. but their language, education, customs, and faith? White America maintains their power and authority based on the cultural ethos of their social development. But this is the blueprint for how every race and ethnic group succeeds.

Without an orientation, African Americans lack the necessary means of establishing unity and cohesiveness to work together on a mass scale. We do not have the social infrastructure to build and maintain our communities as other races of people. It is a direct result of our enslavement as to why we are fragmented and weighed down with divisive beliefs and social entanglements.

Aside from our shades of brown skin and physical features, there is very little about us that says anything African. As a result, we see ourselves as nondescript individuals which lends to our naiveté in viewing the world as a smorgasbord of personal choices. We engage in everyone else's culture but our own. If you were to simply look at religion for example, most White Americans are Christians and the religion reflects its European origins dating back to Constantine and the Roman Catholic Church. Hence, the worldwide image of Jesus as a Jew of European descent.

This is because Christianity is derived from Judaism. In fact, the first five books of Moses are taken from the Jewish Torah. Therefore, God spoke the holy word of the bible in the Hebrew language. In Genesis, the world does not begin according to an African timeframe but with the Jewish calendar because the pyramids in Egypt are 2,000 years older than the story of Adam and Eve. Nevertheless, the holy land is Israel and Jews are "God's chosen people" according to the Christian faith.

Hinduism is one of the oldest religious faiths and it originated in India approximately 2,500 B.C.E. As such, God "Shiva" spoke the holy word in the sacred books of the Vedas and the Bhagavad Gita in the ancient writings of Sanskrit which are commonly translated in the Hindi language. The holy city according to the faith is Varanasi which is in the north east region of India, and Krishna, the Virgin-born savior and deity is of Indian descent.

Islam was founded by the Prophet Muhammad in the 7th century A.C.E. in Saudi Arabia. According to the faith, God "Allah" spoke the holy word of the Quran in the Arabic language. For a Muslim to pray properly, he or she must turn east towards the holy cities of Mecca and Medina. This is a region of Saudi Arabia where Muslims travel to make Hajj which is one of the Five Pillars of Islam.

It goes without saying that every race is serving the same God, but they are doing so from their own cultural perspective. Because religion in general is a form of nationalism and the intent of every nation is to empower its own people. So, we must ask ourselves where is the African concept of God? Where is the God who spoke the holy word in isiZulu, Igbo, Akan, Swahili, or Hausa? What land on the continent did God designate as holy? Is it Johannesburg, Mali, Axum, or Mount Kilimanjaro?

This is to say that if we are not embracing an African concept of God then we are embracing someone else's. Imagine if an entire nation of Japan decided to become Mormons. Their first act would be to consciously reject and abandon their ancestral belief in Shinto. Their actions would say to the world that they see very little merit and validity in their own faith and perceive greater value and truth in someone else's. It would be an outward sign of callous disrespect towards their ancestors and ancient traditions and folly on their behalf. Although our faith was not relinquished as an act of free will, it is necessary that we take it back and reclaim it.

If we as a people of African descent cannot hold our traditional beliefs in high regard, then it is equally inconceivable of others. And it started when we were told in no uncertain terms by the slave master and the colonizer that our beliefs were backwards, and our God was inferior. Our oppression was not just one of physical bondage and restraint, but it was as much psychological in terms of assaulting our self-esteem and dignity and eviscerating our pride to accept an inferior posture without question.

But if McDonald's, Burger King and Wendy's can all sell their own burgers, fries, and drinks then what gives us the impression that we cannot do the same? The masses of African Americans are impoverished, suffering, and dying everyday while other communities continue to thrive and flourish. So, let us not resign ourselves to descriptive terms such as "black", "brown" or "dark" as justification to hold on to a belief that is under the dominance and control of another people. We cannot compromise our dignity to simply see ourselves on the peripheral of someone else's reality. Afterall, faith is a vital component to our orientation.

The greatest of all ironies is that the African faith in ancient Egypt (Kemet) is the oldest concept of religion in the world and it influenced the development of every other faith on the planet. As early as 3400 B.C.E., Abdu, modern day Abydos, was established as the first holy city in recorded history. The oldest spiritual text is carved into the walls of the Temple of Unas, and the Kemetic people coined the term ma'at which means truth, justice, rightness, balance, and reciprocity.

Akhenaton was the first to establish monotheism, the belief in one God, Ra, and the story of Ausar, Aset and Heru is the first story in recorded history of a holy Trinity, royal family, Immaculate Conception, Virgin birth and resurrection. In fact, many of the biblical accounts to include the great flood and the Ten Commandments are direct replicas of Africa's ancient scripts.

Nevertheless, in our community we constantly talk about voting, better housing, healthcare and resources, economic development, jobs, opportunities, racism, and inequality. We are 13% of the U.S. population but 50% of the prison population. The murder rate from black on black crime exceeds a thousand deaths every year and we can never seem to get off this treadmill of misery.

To a large extent, it is our lack of culture and understanding of its significance that prevents us from advancing throughout society. We cannot call ourselves a free people when we are functioning as the cultural stepchildren of White America. While their language, education and religious faith empowers their community, it has left ours disenfranchised, broken, impoverished and depraved. We must remember that no one can look you in the eye if you are choosing to stand beneath them.

For the most part, any amount of success that we enjoy seems to only come about individually but it is never community wide. But Oprah, Michael Jordan, Beyoncé, and a handful of celebrities do not begin to tell the story of the harsh realities of urban life. So, the question becomes how do we develop and establish our own cultural orientation to empower African Americans?

Here is an outline for us to follow:

The first six months should consist of reading these four books and reviewing them afterwards:

1. The Autobiography of Malcolm X
2. Chains and Images of Psychological Slavery by Dr. Na'im Akbar
3. Nile Valley Contributions to Civilization by Tony Browder
4. The Rage of a Privilege Class by Ellis Cose

In addition to reading the books we should celebrate Kwanzaa every year starting on December 26th through January 1st. This means it is essential to read Dr. Maulana Karenga's book on the holiday to familiarize yourself with the festivities, outline, and structure.

We must do the same on Juneteenth each year. We must honor and celebrate the 19th of June as our day of Independence.   This celebration is more of a family and communal gathering that we can plan with the members of our own communities.

At the very least, patronize a black-owned business once a month. Whether it is a hair salon, barber shop, book or clothing store, restaurant, product, or service, it is important that we give back and do so in good faith. When we support our own businesses, it allows us to employ the people in our own communities. Which in turn helps to lift our people out of poverty and debt. We must remember that Kemet was not built in a day, and every contribution is invaluable.

Next, we must continue to read to reeducate ourselves, expand our knowledgebase and raise our conscious awareness. We should commit ourselves to reading no less than four books a year and they should primarily be the work from the following scholars in no particular order:

- John Henrik Clarke: <u>Christopher Columbus and the Afrikan Holocaust</u>; African People in World History; <u>Critical Lessons in Slavery and the Slavetrade</u>
- Ben Jochannan: Black Man of the Nile and His Family; African Origins of the Major Western Religions; <u>New Dimensions in African History</u>; The Black Man's Religion

- Cheikh Anta Diop: <u>The African Origins of Civilization</u>; Civilization or Barbarism; Black Africa; The Cultural Unity of Black Africa
- Molefi Kete Asante: Afrocentricity; The History of Africa; 400 Years of Witnessing; Encyclopedia of African Religion; The Afrocentric Idea
- Maulana Karenga: <u>Kwanzaa</u>; Kawaida and Questions of Life and Struggle; The Husia; Odu Ifa; Maat, the Moral Ideal in Ancient Egypt
- Francis Cress Welsing: The Isis Papers; <u>The Cress Theory of Color confrontation</u>
- Chancellor Williams: <u>The Destruction of Black Civilization</u>; Rebirth of African Civilization
- Amos Wilson: <u>Blueprint for Black Power</u>; Awaking the Natural Genius of Black Children; The Developmental Psychology of the Black Child; African-Centered Consciousness Versus the New World Order; <u>Black on Black Violence</u>
- Ivan Van Sertima: <u>They Came Before Columbus</u>; <u>Blacks In Science</u>; Golden Age of the Moor; Nile Valley Civilizations; Egypt Revisited
- John G. Jackson: <u>Christianity Before Christ</u>; Introduction to African Civilizations; Ethiopia and the Origin of Civilization
- Leonard Jeffries: The African American's Search for Truth and Knowledge
- George GM James: <u>Stolen Legacy: Greek Philosophy is Stolen Egyptian Philosophy</u>
- Wade Nobles: <u>Seeking the Sakhu</u>; African Psychology; Island of Memes
- Marimba Ani: <u>Let the Circle Be Unbroken</u>; Yurugu

- Charles S. Finch III: Echoes of the Old Dark Land; The Star of Deep Beginnings; <u>The African Background to Medical Science</u>; Africa and the Birth of Science and Technology
- Runoko Rashidi: Black Star; <u>African Presence in Early Asia</u>
- Theophile Obenga: Ancient Egypt and Black Africa
- Carter G. Woodson: <u>The Miseducation of the Negro</u>
- Jacob Carruthers: Intellectual Warfare; African world History Project
- Chinweizu: West and the Rest of Us
- Asa Hilliard: The Maroon Within Us; SBA: The Reawakening of the African Mind
- Na'im Akbar: <u>Chains and Images of Psychological Slavery</u>; <u>Know Thy Self</u>; <u>Visions for Black Men</u>
- Tony Browder: <u>From the Browder File</u>; <u>Nile Valley Contributions to Civilization</u>; <u>Survival Strategies for Africans in America</u>
- Michelle Alexander: <u>The New Jim Crow</u>
- Ellis Cose: <u>Rage of A Privileged Class</u>
- Chinua Achebe: <u>Things Fall Apart</u>
- Frantz Fanon: Black Skin, White Masks
- Jawanza Kunjufu: <u>Countering the Conspiracy to Destroy Black Boys</u>; Developing Positive Self-images & Discipline in Black Children

Some of the books are more difficult to read than others so I have underlined the ones that I would recommend if you are just starting out. And this is not to say that other books on the Black experience are not important, but this list is the core of our necessary reading material. Understand that our scholars have dedicated most of their lives in studying our history and risked their professional careers by telling us a truth that most people do not want us to know. Therefore, it is imperative that we read their work with respect and due diligence.

In addition, there are some powerful songs from soulful artists that are recommended. Music that touches the spirit of struggle. Some of the artists are Denise Williams (Black Butterfly), James Brown (Say It Loud, I'm Black and I'm Proud), Indie Arie, Soul II Soul, Bob Marley, Curtis Mayfield, Public Enemy, Nina Simone, Kool Moe Dee (Knowledge Is King), KRS-One, Peter Tosh, Billie Holiday (Strange Fruit). There is a host of other songs and artists that have positively contributed to our cause with soul-inspiring and uplifting messages.

For those of us who commit to an orientation, if we are thorough, open, and receptive, we will start to build and grow small units of conscious people throughout our communities. In fact, they will join those of us who are already in the movement. And as we continue, it will slowly spread into the larger areas. It may realistically take several years just in the initial phase alone, but you will soon see small steps of improvement as changes occur.

It will be evident in the academic performance of the children with conscious parents. It will be recognized in the responsible behavior and actions of our adults and in the money generated by black owned businesses. It will be in the reduction of crime, police presence and abuse of power, not to mention cleaner communities, better jobs and opportunities with less drugs and alcohol. This will be the start of a new beginning as the bata drum continues.

More Inspiring Thoughts

Always do your best. What you plant now, you will harvest later
– Og Mandigo

Where we put our awareness, and for how long, maps our destiny - Dr. Joe Dispenza

One minute of anger weakens your immune system for 4 to 5 hours. One minute of laughter boosts your immune system for over 24 hours – Olivia

"Peace is the beauty of life. It is sunshine. It is the smile of a child, the love of a mother, the joy of a father, the togetherness of a family. It is the advancement of man, the victory of a just cause, the triumph of truth." – Menachem Begin

A lie can travel halfway around the world while the truth is putting on its shoes – Charles Spurgeon

"Mindfulness is the process of actively noticing new things. When you do that, it puts you in the present. It makes you more sensitive to context and perspective. It's the essence of engagement." – Ellen Langer

Feeling is the language that speaks to the Universe. Feel as though your goal is accomplished and your prayer is already answered – Gregg Braden

The greatest achievement is selflessness...

The greatest worth is self-mastery...

The greatest quality is seeking to serve others...

The greatest precept is continued awareness...

The greatest medicine is the emptiness of everything...

The greatest action is not conforming with the world ways...

The greatest magic is transmuting the passions...

The greatest generosity is non-attachment...

The greatest goodness is a peaceful mind...

The greatest patience is humility...

The greatest effort is not concerned with results...

The greatest meditation is a mind that lets go...

The greatest wisdom is seeing through appearances." –
Buddhist quotes

The mind and the body are like parallel universes. Anything that happens in the mental universe must leave tracks in the physical one – Dr. Deepak Chopra

Yesterday I was clever, so I wanted to change the world. Today I am wise, so I am changing myself- Rumi

Expect nothing and you will never be disappointed – author unknown

A ship is always safe at shore but that is not what it's built for – Albert Einstein

Determination is the wake-up call to the human will – Tony Robbins

When I let go of what I am, I become what I might be – Lao Tzu

If you can't fly then run, if you can't run then walk, if you can't walk then crawl, but whatever you do you have to keep moving forward – Dr. Martin Luther King, Jr.

When the power of love overcomes the love of power, the world will know peace – Jimi Hendrix

Change will not come if we wait for some other person or some other time. We are the ones we've been waiting for. We are the change that we seek – Barack Obama

People who are crazy enough to think they can change the world are the ones who do – Steve Jobs

Minds are like parachutes, they only function when they are open – James Dewar

"As my friend and I were passing the elephants, he suddenly stopped, confused by the fact that these huge creatures were being held by only a small rope tied to their front leg. No chains, no cages. It was obvious that the elephants could, at any time, break away from the ropes they were tied to but for some reason, they did not. My friend saw a trainer nearby and asked why these beautiful, magnificent animals just stood there and made no attempt to get away.

"Well", he said, "when they are very young and much smaller, we use the same size rope to tie them and, at that age, it's enough to hold them. As they grow up, they are conditioned to believe they cannot break away. They believe the rope can still hold them, so they never try to break free." My friend was amazed. These animals could at any time break free from their bonds but because they believed they couldn't, they were stuck right where they were." – author unknown